An Introduction to

Northern California Birds

Herbert Clarke

Photographs by the Author

Mountain Press Publishing Company
Missoula, Montana
1995

JUN 1 4 1996

© Copyright 1995 by Herbert Clarke

Front cover photo: Western Tanager, male
Back cover photo: California Quail, female

Second Printing, January 1996

Library of Congress Cataloging-in-Publication Data

Clarke, Herbert, 1927–
 An introduction to Northern California birds / Herbert Clarke :
photographs by the author.
  p. cm.
 Includes bibliographical references (p.   ) and index.
 ISBN 0-87842-312-5
 1. Birds—California, Northern—Identification. 2. Birds—
California, Northern—Pictorial works. I. Title.
QL684.C2C564 1995   95-2055
598.29794—dc20   CIP

Printed in Hong Kong by Mantec Production Company

Mountain Press Publishing Company
P. O. Box 2399 • Missoula, Montana 59806
(406) 728-1900 • (800) 234-5308

To Olga—my continuing inspiration!

Contents

Acknowledgments

I am deeply grateful to many people who have shared their knowledge, expertise, and enjoyable company with me over the years. The indirect contributions of three friends especially stand out: Clyde Bergman, Larry Sansone, and Arnold Small. We have spent many pleasant hours traveling together and discussing every subject under the sun, including, of course, birds. Our severe but friendly critique of each others' pictures has greatly improved my photography. Together, we have participated in many memorable nature experiences. I am also indebted to the many people who have found my earlier book useful in adding to their understanding of southern California's birdlife and who encouraged me to write about the rest of this marvelous state.

Kathleen Ort, John De Roo, and Kim Pryhorocki of Mountain Press Publishing Company have been invaluable with their advice, patience, and cooperation in the production of this book. Rich Stallcup, whose knowledge of northern California's birdlife is unequaled, carefully reviewed the text and made many excellent suggestions regarding style and content. Kimball Garrett, a keen observer and prolific writer about California birdlife, patiently helped further refine the text and peruse the pictures for accuracy. However, I take full responsibility for any errors, which I hope are few. Many thanks are extended to Debra Shearwater, whose excellent pelagic birding operations afforded me many opportunities to observe and photograph oceanic wildlife. Without Jack Wilburn's system of photographic lighting, I would have been unable to obtain many of the pictures used in this book. The encouragement and critical overview by my wife, Olga, have been particularly helpful. The excellent map of northern California was produced by Jonathan Alderfer, one of California's finest bird artists.

My quest to capture wild birds well on film has given me great satisfaction for over 40 years. It is been especially gratifying to share some of my experiences with a great number of people. On occasion, even after all this time, some of my feathered friends have still managed to elude my photographic efforts. This continuing challenge has intensified my enjoyment and appreciation of all creatures with which we share this planet.

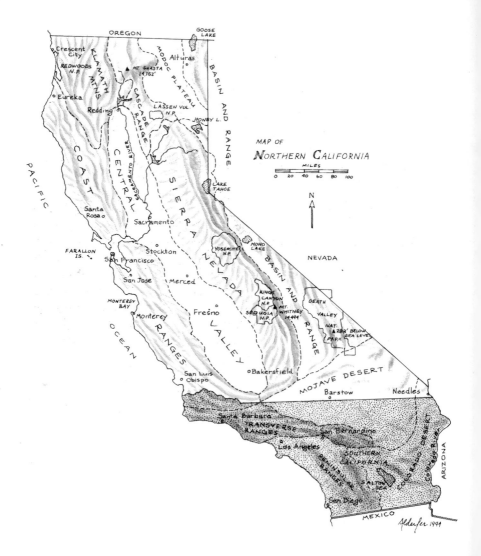

OREGON

GOOSE
LAKE

Crescent
City

REDWOODS
N.P.

KLAMATH MTNS

MODOC PLATEAU

Alturas

MT. SHASTA
14,162'

CASCADE RANGE

Eureka

Redding

LASSEN VOL.
N.P.

HONEY L.

BASIN AND RANGE

MAP OF

NORTHERN CALIFORNIA

MILES
0   20 40 60 80 100

N

COAST

SACRAMENTO RIVER

CENTRAL

SIERRA

LAKE
TAHOE

Santa
Rosa

Sacramento

FARALLON
IS.

Stockton

San Francisco

NEVADA

YOSEMITE
N.P.

MONO
LAKE

San Jose

Merced

NEVADA

BASIN AND RANGE

MONTEREY
BAY

Monterey

VALLEY

Fresno

KINGS
CANYON
N.P.

SEQUOIA
N.P.

MT.
WHITNEY
14,494'

DEATH

VALLEY

NAT.

PARK

282' BELOW
SEA LEVEL

OCEAN

RANGES

San Luis
Obispo

Bakersfield

MOJAVE DESERT

Barstow

Needles

Santa Barbara

TRANSVERSE
RANGES

San Bernardino

Los Angeles

PENINSULAR RANGES

SOUTHERN
CALIFORNIA

SALTON
SEA

COLORADO DESERT

COLORADO R.

ARIZONA

San Diego

MEXICO

Aldenfer 1991

PACIFIC

Northern California

This book covers California from the Oregon border south to the northern boundary of Santa Barbara County and eastward through mid-San Bernardino County.

Northern California is even more ecologically complex than southern California (see the companion book, *An Introduction to Southern California Birds*). The region's human population ranges from the high density of the San Francisco Bay area to some of the least populated spaces of the state. Rainfall varies tremendously from the wettest portions (northwest coastal sections and high mountains) to the driest (Great Basin deserts). Another variable is altitude, which ranges from the heights of the Sierra Nevada (over 14,000 feet) down to Death Valley (more than 200 feet below sea level), with corresponding extremes in temperature. The mixture of dissimilar habitats in close proximity to each other contributes to the diversity of birdlife. Complex movements of birds are influenced by such variables as season, weather, and food supply.

Introduction

I am gratified by the excellent reception received by *An Introduction to Southern California Birds*, first published in 1989. This book follows the same format as its southern California predecessor. Included here are accounts of a number of additional species as well as new photographs and descriptions of birds illustrated in the earlier work. Each book stands alone, but together they should enable the casual birder to identify most birds encountered in the state.

My aim is to introduce interested beginners to the wonderful world of birds inhabiting one of the great natural regions of the earth—northern California. California's natural beauty and generally pleasant climate make it one of the best places in the world to enjoy the out-of-doors. Good roads and diverse habitats relatively close to one another have created an awareness and appreciation of the state's natural environment, and especially its birdlife, in a growing segment of residents and visitors. Where else can one quickly visit, almost year-round, such varied major habitats as ocean, mountains, and deserts, interspersed with a myriad of lesser ecosystems? This diversity is reflected in the variety and abundance of birds, which in turn has resulted in California having perhaps a larger number of active birders than any other state.

Birds, because of their ability to fly with seemingly no earthly restraints, combined with their bright colors and remarkable habits, have long fascinated humans. Birds are the most conspicuous form of wildlife encountered by the majority of people, which has led to bird-watching or birding (the preferred term) becoming a more and more popular hobby nationally.

Everyone likes to apply a name, without too much difficulty, to the creature they are viewing. There is a huge variety of books available covering every aspect of ornithology (the study of birds). The problem is that just about all of them urge the keeping of careful notes or are too detailed and technical for the casual or beginning birder.

It is possible for the resident or visitor to California to observe and name most of our marvelous birds without delving deeply into taxonomy (the study of the scientific classification of plants and animals) or any of the other technical aspects of ornithology. It is enough to enjoy these innocent creatures for their own sake, enabling the observer, for the moment, to lay aside worldly cares.

Hermit Thrush at dripping faucet

Identifying Birds

What defines a bird? Not its ability to fly. Insects, mammals (bats), even fish can take to the air, while some birds cannot. The definitive characteristic of all birds is the presence of feathers. If the creature has feathers, it is a bird. If it does not, it is some other kind of organism.

The natural history of northern California is too complicated to describe in detail here. In order to provide some understanding of this diverse region, I have arbitrarily divided the area into six broad divisions and included typical birds that can commonly be found therein. When attempting to identify a particular bird, take into account its habitat and locality. If you cannot find the particular bird under observation in a certain chapter, look through some of the other sections in which it might be included. Precise arrangement of birds in definitive habitats is difficult because many species can regularly be found in several, sometimes quite different, areas. This book is not a complete field guide, so you may need to consult one of the references listed in the back for more information.

Overall lengths are shown in inches, measured from bill tip to tail tip. This can be misleading, especially in species with long bills such as thrashers, hummingbirds, or shorebirds. Even a small variation is exaggerated by build (stocky or slender). Overall size does not necessarily indicate the age of a bird. In most species, a recently fledged (having left the nest) young bird is about the same size as its fully grown parents, although there may be further plumage changes as the bird becomes a breeding adult. Remember this when attempting to identify birds of similar appearance. Also, plumage may vary with season, gender, and age. When appropriate, these differences are mentioned in the text. Otherwise, it can be assumed there is no apparent plumage variation between sexes. Songs and calls are difficult to describe; words can convey only a general impression of bird vocalizations. Keep this in mind when listening to a bird. With practice, most species can be identified by their songs or calls.

General Information

All birds usually have more than one name—at least one common name and a scientific one. The latter is used when referring to species among professional ornithologists, and appellations in other languages are used in various parts of the world. In this book, species arrangement and names follow the American Ornithologists' Union *Check-list of North American Birds,* sixth edition, and subsequent supplements.

Exotic birds of unknown origin are often observed in northern California. These include parrots and ducks as well as flamingos, peafowl, and certain finches. Some may have escaped from captivity

Anna's Hummingbirds at feeder

during shipping or while being kept as pets, and others were deliberately released. They survive because of mild climate and easily obtainable food, but usually do not multiply and expand their range. These exotic birds, with only a few exceptions, are not discussed in this book.

A good binocular is of great help in perceiving subtle details of plumage. Buy the highest quality you can afford. A fine camera store or a reliable retailer familiar with the unique requirements of birders can suggest which kind of binocular is best for your need and purse.

Should you wish to learn more about birds, there are many ways to gain knowledge and skill. The suggested references at the back of this book can lead you to information sources to further your study. You might consider joining a local Audubon Society or similar nature organization.

There is no correct or precise way to study birds. Individual interests and skills vary widely. It is a personal decision how deeply one wants to become involved in this fascinating endeavor. Relax and enjoy yourself at whatever level you desire to participate.

Attracting Birds

An effective way to attract birds to home gardens is to provide a suitable source for water, protected from cats, along with some planting for cover. Water can come from a drip of some kind, such as a slow-running or leaky faucet. Elaborate birdbaths are fine but unnecessary, and it is imperative to keep a birdbath clean by changing the water frequently. Foods that lure birds include chicken scratch, bread crumbs, peanut butter, suet, wild-bird seed, and sunflower seeds. Various commercial feeders are available, but a suitable homemade one usually works well. Water, food, and sugar-water feeders can attract many feathered visitors, allowing them to constantly delight you for little cost and effort. Feeding stations should be kept clean, sheltered, and catproof. Landscaping with fruiting and berry-bearing trees and shrubs is an excellent way to draw birds. A local garden nursery can advise you on which plants are best suited to your area. Sometimes you can entice birds to nest by proper construction, placement, and maintenance of birdhouses or bird boxes. Try trial-and-error techniques or perhaps consult reference material at your local library.

White-breasted Nuthatch at suet feeder

San Francisco from Marin County

City park, Santa Clara County

Chapter I
Birds of Cities and Towns

Included here are densely populated areas of the state such as San Francisco and the Bay Area, Sacramento, Fresno, Monterey, and other cities and towns. Surprisingly, a large number of birds can be found in these jungles of steel and concrete. Downtown areas have abundant Rock Doves, House Sparrows, and European Starlings, all non-native species, augmented by House Finches, gulls, and other native birds taking advantage of food, water, and shelter incidentally provided by humans.

Most people are unaware of the richness of birdlife in an urban setting. Tree-lined streets, parks, landfills, golf courses, and gardens all add to an artificial environment occupied by opportunistic birdlife. Availability of water where it's not found naturally may attract birds far from their normal habitats. Depending on food and water sources, desert and mountain species can often appear, while large numbers of other birds regularly migrate through cities and towns in spring and fall on their way to northern nesting grounds or southerly wintering regions. Some years, especially in winter, because of unusual weather conditions or an abundance of preferred food, there is an irruption in numbers of some mountain species that come into cities and lowlands. Among these birds are robins, waxwings, nuthatches, finches, jays, and even woodpeckers. Factors such as local climate, proximity to bodies of water, amount of development, and both native and exotic plantings affect the number of species in urban settings.

Unrestricted development has destroyed several unique habitats where birds with specialized requirements have had their numbers greatly reduced or have even been extirpated. Examples are marshland (Clapper Rail) and riparian woodlands (Yellow-billed Cuckoo).

Birds in cities brighten an otherwise bleak landscape, and even the casual observer enriches his or her life by becoming aware of our feathered coinhabitants while pursuing everyday activities. An added advantage to living in California's urban areas is that they are hubs of excellent road systems, enabling people with limited time and money to easily escape into a variety of close-by habitats.

Mallard
Anas platyrhynchos 23"

This is a familiar park duck seen in urban areas. Most individuals observed in these places are released captive birds, although there may be a few genuine wild birds attracted by the domesticated ones. Many strange combinations of plumage and color result from interbreeding of tame stock with wild individuals. Wild Mallards are common in winter in wet habitats throughout California, with the greatest breeding concentrations in Canada's prairie provinces of Alberta, Saskatchewan, and Manitoba. Nests are constructed on the ground in reeds or tall grass near water, and up to 12 light green eggs are laid. The young are able to leave the nest, walk, and swim almost immediately upon hatching. Food consists primarily of various aquatic plants but sometimes includes insects, snails, and even dead fish. In parks these ducks are fond of birdseed and bread. Females are mostly brown.

American Coot
Fulica americana 15½"

Coots are often mistakenly called ducks, but they are really members of the rail family. They can swim and dive as well as ducks because their toes have flat, fleshy lobes that aid in paddling much like the webs that join the toes of ducks. This abundant bird, nicknamed "mudhen," is found in all kinds of wetlands. In urban settings, it likes to graze in grassy areas and on golf course greens, where it is often considered a pest. Coots build floating nests anchored to growing plants and lay about 10 pinkish, black-spotted eggs. They are quarrelsome, noisy birds with calls consisting mainly of croaks and squawks. Coots eat a variety of plant and animal life, including grass, grain, insects, worms, and small fish.

Rock Dove
Columba livia 12½"

This park pigeon is one of the most familiar birds in cities and even in the countryside. It was introduced to North America from Europe and Asia. Selective breeding of captive birds has resulted in many plumage variations and colors. Normal coloration of wild Rock Doves is similar to that of the bird pictured here. Natural nesting sites are on rocky cliffs and hillsides, but in California they have been augmented by buildings and bridges. These doves are prolific breeders, and their population is restricted only by predators such as hawks and by their food supply, which is greatly supplemented by people.

Mallard, male

American Coot with chick

Rock Dove

Mourning Dove
Zenaida macroura 12"

Mourning Doves are the most abundant and widespread of our native doves. Their name is derived from their mournful cooing call, and they also make a distinctive whirring sound with their wings when flying. Habitats include countryside, desert, and open forest, as well as shrubby sections of cities. These doves do not migrate, although there is considerable shifting of local populations due to weather and food supply. Two white eggs are laid in a flimsy nest, built anywhere from ground level to high in trees. Doves are strictly seed eaters.

Barn Owl
Tyto alba 16"

Barn Owls are found nearly worldwide in temperate and tropical regions. They are usually nocturnal but occasionally, when disturbed, will fly about in the daytime. Nesting sites are located in dark, sheltered places such as palm trees, barns, mine shafts, caves, belfries, and burrows. Food consists of mice, rats, and rabbits; like most owls, Barn Owls regurgitate indigestible bones and fur in the form of pellets. A combination of excellent night vision and keen hearing allows owls to locate prey during the darkest of nights. Barn Owls' silent flight, pale coloration, and harsh hissing calls combine to present a ghostly appearance, especially in poor light. Populations of these birds in California have greatly declined because of widespread development.

Northern Flicker
Colaptes auratus 12½"

Conspicuous reddish flight feathers combined with a white rump make this woodpecker easy to identify. Plumages of the sexes are similar, with males having red mustache marks. Its varied diet includes berries and fruit, ants and grubs picked from the ground, and insects probed from tree bark. Some populations of flickers migrate, but others do not. Many mountain birds simply retreat to lower altitudes in the winter. High dead snags in open parks and woodlands are preferred nesting sites. Flickers often perch and drum on trees and utility poles, occasionally becoming a nuisance when they drill into wooden buildings.

Mourning Dove

Barn Owl

Northern Flicker, male

White-throated Swift
Aeronautes saxatalis 6½"

Swifts are often confused with swallows because of similarity of flight. However, they belong to entirely unrelated groups. White-throated Swifts do not migrate and are found over a wide range of habitats. They fly at great heights, catching insects on the wing while covering tremendous distances. Swifts are among the world's fastest fliers. Crevices in sheer cliffs are their normal nesting sites, but in built-up areas they utilize crannies in buildings and concrete bridges. These locations offer excellent protection from predators. Nests consist of feathers and grasses cemented together with the swift's saliva and glued to a flat vertical surface. They lay four or five white eggs. Swifts may become torpid (inactive) during periods of cool weather when flying insects are unavailable.

Scrub Jay
Aphelocoma coerulescens 11½"

This bird is often mistakenly called the Blue Jay, a crested jay found in the eastern United States. The Scrub Jay is a year-round resident of California in brushy areas from sea level up to lower mountain elevations. This jay is noisy and aggressive but can become tame enough to take food from the hand. It is especially fond of peanuts. Nests are composed of sticks lined with rootlets and are well hidden in dense, low trees or bushes. Four to six speckled eggs are laid, and young leave the nest about 18 days after hatching. The Scrub Jay's diet is varied and includes acorns, insects, seeds, mice, and sometimes the eggs and young of smaller birds.

White-throated Swift, perched

White-throated Swift in flight

Scrub Jay

Anna's Hummingbird
Calypte anna 4"

This is the most familiar California hummingbird. It is often misidentified as the Ruby-throated Hummingbird, a species found only in the eastern United States that does not have red extending to the top of the head. Color is often difficult to perceive in hummingbirds because hues are produced by the physical structure of the feather rather than by true feather pigments. Anna's Hummingbirds feed on flower nectar as well as insects, soft fruit, and even certain kinds of sap. The nesting season is extended, lasting from midwinter to midsummer. As is characteristic of all North American hummingbirds, females do all the work of building nests, laying and incubating two white eggs, and raising young. Female and immature male hummingbirds of most species lack the adult male Anna's brilliant gorget (throat and head areas) and are dingy white below, usually with only a suggestion of throat color. Males' songs mostly consist of a series of loud squeaks. They guard their feeding territories with spectacular pendulum-like aerial exhibitions, aggressively chasing away other hummingbirds. When displaying to females, they dive toward them at tremendous speed and at the bottom of the plunge emit a sharp *peek*.

American Crow
Corvus brachyrhynchos 17½"

Crows are close relatives of ravens and jays and like those birds can be bold and aggressive, though they are usually wary of people. They have become common in suburban and rural areas, preferring open woods and parks. Crows are similar in appearance to ravens, but are smaller and do not soar as much. Nests are well built of twigs lined with soft materials including plant fibers, moss, leaves, and sometimes rags. Nest locations range from low dense hedges to high in trees. Crows are scavengers and will eat almost anything but prefer grains, seeds, and nuts. In some cultivated areas, these birds are considered pests and have been poisoned and shot in large numbers because of alleged crop damage. But in spite of this persecution, crows easily persist by wit and adaptability to local conditions.

Anna's Hummingbird, male

Anna's Hummingbird, female on nest

American Crow

Plain Titmouse

Parus inornatus 5¾"

Titmice are California's smallest birds with crests. Their principal habitat is open oak woodlands, where they make their nests in old woodpecker holes, natural tree cavities, and small openings in man-made structures. Titmice are acrobatic, often clinging upside down on tree limbs while foraging for insects. They will also eat seeds and fruit and are easily attracted to feeders. These small birds are year-round residents in most of their habitat. Pairs have a tendency to remain mated for at least two years. Males sing persistently in the spring, whistling *weety weety weety*.

House Wren

Troglodytes aedon 4¾"

These diminutive wrens make their presence known by their loud, exuberant songs. They are common in residential areas and woodlands with brushy understories, especially in the Central Valley, its surrounding foothills, and the Great Basin. Adults almost invariably return to localities where they previously nested to again build in small natural or man-made cavities. They vigorously defend their territories, often attacking the eggs and nests of not only intruding House Wrens but other species as well. Clutches commonly consist of six to eight white eggs with brown speckles. Food is almost entirely insects. The winter range is from southern California to Mexico.

American Robin

Turdus migratorius 10"

This species is perhaps the best-known native bird in the United States. It is often seen in gardens busily searching for earthworms and insects. Robins are also fond of fruits and berries. Nests, containing three to five blue, unmarked eggs, are built anywhere from near ground level to the tops of tall trees and even in buildings. Two broods are often raised per season. Females are paler than males, and young have spotted breasts, as is typical of the thrush family. This bird is common throughout northern California in humid open woodlands. As winter approaches, robins move from mountains into lower elevations and from north to south, sometimes gathering in large flocks in search of berries.

Plain Titmouse

House Wren

American Robin, male

European Starling
Sturnus vulgaris 8½"

Starlings are native to Europe and were introduced into eastern North America in the late nineteenth century. Since then, they have spread rapidly west across the continent and are now common in virtually every city and town in California, as well as in most cultivated areas. In many urban regions their large numbers have created noise and dirt problems, while in other places their aggressive, opportunistic behavior has caused sharp declines in numbers of native birds, especially hole-nesting species. Starlings nest in woodpecker holes, rock crevices, and buildings, usually laying five light blue eggs. Their song is a variety of loud whistles and squeaks, but they are capable of imitating the vocalizations of other birds. After nesting, adults molt into a prominently spotted and somewhat less glossy plumage, with the yellow bill turning dark. Insects, grain, and food scraps are usually obtained from the ground.

Northern Mockingbird
Mimus polyglottos 10"

The mockingbird's continuous exuberant singing, day and night from tall perches, is a delight to most people but an annoyance to some. These birds are expert mimics of other birds' songs and will also imitate barking dogs, squeaking wheels, whistles, and many other sounds. They can be attracted to gardens by berry-bearing shrubs, water, and food such as raisins and bread. Large quantities of insects also are consumed. Nests are built in low, dense shrubs or trees, and four to five young are raised. Mockingbirds inhabit lower elevations wherever there are scattered trees and brush near human dwellings. Flashing white wing patches and white outer tail feathers, combined with their joyous songs, make mockingbirds a year-round captivating addition to many communities.

Cedar Waxwing
Bombycilla cedrorum 7¼"

In California these birds breed only in the northwest, moving south throughout most of the state after nesting. Winter numbers can vary widely, depending on weather and food supply, as legions of individuals from more northerly states and Canada move southward. The sleek, silky plumage, often combined with waxy, bright red tips on the inner wing feathers, give this species its unusual name. Waxwings are one of our few birds with prominent crests. Flocks gather to feed on berries of all kinds, often passing them from bird to bird. They also eat insects and sap. Their song is a simple, short, very high-pitched trill.

European Starling

Northern Mockingbird,
adult at nest with nestlings

Cedar Waxwing

California Towhee
Pipilo crissalis 8½"

Until recently, California Towhees were named Brown Towhees. They were separated from another similar species, resident in the southern Rocky Mountain region, based on subtle differences in behavior, voice, and body structure. Towhees are not wary and are a familiar sight in brushy areas in and around human habitations. Nests are built in dense bushes and low trees. The four pale blue eggs are spotted with black, and often two broods a year are raised. California Towhees scratch on the ground for seeds and insects. They are easily attracted to feeders by peanut butter and wild-bird feed. Their song is an abrupt series of sharp notes on one pitch that quickens to a trill.

Golden-crowned Sparrow
Zonotrichia atricapilla 7"

These sparrows are winter visitors only, nesting in western Canada and Alaska. Adult winter feathering is similar to that of the immature illustrated; in spring, just before returning to the north, both young and mature birds begin to attain their breeding plumage, mainly consisting of a heavy black band over each eye and an intense yellow crown. Golden-crowns forage on the ground for seeds in small flocks that sometimes include other species of sparrows. They readily come to seed feeders. Winter habitats are thick brush and borders of oak and streamside woodlands. Their musical song, heard in early spring, consists of three high-pitched, clearly whistled descending notes.

White-crowned Sparrow
Zonotrichia leucophrys 7"

White-crowned Sparrows are common winter visitors, with additional populations breeding in the narrow, humid coastal belt, the northeastern mountains, and the higher regions of the Sierra Nevada. There are several forms or "subspecies" of this sparrow, each differing slightly in the head pattern. Immature birds, seen in the winter, have head markings consisting of reddish brown stripes on a buffy crown. Food consists mainly of seeds along with some berries. White-crowns often feed and travel in flocks of mixed species of sparrows in a variety of habitats from brushy fields to open woodlands. Its pretty song of some half a dozen high-pitched, musical notes and wheezy trills can be heard throughout the year.

California Towhee

Golden-crowned Sparrow, fall immature

White-crowned Sparrow

Brewer's Blackbird

Euphagus cyanocephalus 9"

Brewer's Blackbirds are found virtually throughout California and are a common sight in city parks and lawns as well as on farms, frequently near water. They tend to travel in flocks and nest in colonies. Females and young are grayish brown and have dark eyes. In the fall, the plumages of molting immature males are splotched with black. Nests, made of a mixture of mud and grass, are lined with fine material such as rootlets and horsehair and built in bushes and trees, often near human habitations. Food consists of grain, seeds, and insects. Their songs are similar to those of other blackbirds, consisting of a mixture of hoarse and musical notes. The call, often given in flight, is an unmusical *chack*.

Northern Oriole

Icterus galbula 8¾"

These orioles mainly spend the winter in Mexico and Central America, with a few overwintering in California. Females resemble first-spring males but lack the black throat. Breeding habitat is in moist deciduous woodlands in suburban areas and the countryside. Nests are made of fine grass woven into a pouch and hung from tree branches. Pairs vigorously defend their nests from egg-eating birds such as magpies and jays. Their natural food is mostly insects, nectar, and berries, but these orioles also are attracted to hummingbird feeders. The song is a loud, flutelike warble consisting of a series of clear, sharp, single and double notes. Older books refer to this bird as Bullock's Oriole, but it is now considered to be the same species as the Baltimore Oriole of eastern North America, with both being called Northern Oriole.

Brewer's Blackbird, male

Northern Oriole, adult male

Northern Oriole, first-spring male

House Finch   *Carpodacus mexicanus 6"*

Native House Finches compete successfully for nesting sites with introduced House Sparrows, somewhat restricting the spread of the sparrow in California. This finch has adapted so well to the works of humans that it has become one of our most familiar birds and is found everywhere except in high mountains. It nests in a great variety of places, including building eaves, flower boxes, old bird nests, vines, and shrubs. Four or five eggs are usually laid and are light blue with black spots. Their nests have a messy appearance because, unlike other species, House Finches do not carry away nestling waste. Plumages of adult males range from bright red to orange. Females and young males are mainly brown with brown-streaked underparts. These finches do not migrate but tend to congregate in large flocks during fall and winter. Their regular diet consists of grain and fruit, and they will readily come to seed and hummingbird feeders. Their melodious song consists of a series of loud, high-pitched warbles run together.

House Sparrow   *Passer domesticus 6¼"*

Formerly known as English Sparrows, House Sparrows have spread over much of North America since their introduction from England in the middle of the nineteenth century. They are year-round residents, almost always near human habitation. Nests, loosely constructed of grass, paper, feathers, and other materials, are usually placed in nooks and crannies of buildings. Occasionally, these birds will build a round dome-shaped nest in a tree or shrub. Their diet is varied, ranging from seeds, berries, and insects to food scraps. Females and young are dull brown above and paler below and lack the male's black throat and bib. Active, noisy flocks of House Sparrows brighten otherwise drab sections of cities where they may be the only birdlife in evidence.

House Finches, female and male

House Finch, nest and nestlings

House Sparrow, male

Listed below are additional birds, discussed in other chapters, that are frequently observed in cities and towns. This is not an all-inclusive list because numbers and varieties can change due to local conditions.

Species	*Preferred Locality*
Pied-billed Grebe	lakes and ponds
Double-crested Cormorant	lakes and reservoirs
American Wigeon	lakes and estuaries
Canvasback	lakes and ponds
Turkey Vulture	soaring overhead
California Quail	brush
Killdeer	grassy areas, fields
California Gull	park ponds and dumps
Glaucous-winged Gull	coast, lakes, and rubbish dumps
Band-tailed Pigeon	wooded suburbs
Great Horned Owl	wooded suburbs
Black Phoebe	streams and ponds
Bushtit	suburbs
American Pipit	grassy areas and lake edges
Western Meadowlark	grassy areas and fields
Red-winged Blackbird	parks and lake margins
Brown-headed Cowbird	gardens
American Goldfinch	suburban parks and gardens
Song Sparrow	moist parks and gardens

Farmland, San Joaquin County

Remnant of natural habitat, Merced County

Chapter II
Birds of the Central Valley

This great valley encompassing the Sacramento and San Joaquin Valleys is essentially a large plain or prairie bounded by mountain ranges. It extends some 450 miles from near Bakersfield in the south to Redding in the north and is as much as 80 miles wide. There is no other flat area of comparable size west of the Rocky Mountains. Summers are hot and dry, while winters are generally mild except in some shaded, narrow valleys where temperatures can drop to well below freezing. Yearly precipitation varies from about 35 inches around Redding to about 7 inches near Bakersfield, with most rain occurring between December and February. Dense fog (called "tule fog") is common during the winter. Most of California's agricultural crops are produced here, and many parts of the valley are heavily irrigated, especially in the southern portion.

The Central Valley is not a uniform natural ecosystem—rather it contains a number of pocket or micro habitats where many of the bird species discussed in other chapters may be observed, depending on season and availability of food and water. Before human settlement, this valley contained a variety of natural habitats, including marshes, grasslands, savannas, streamside woodlands, and elements of desert. Intensive development has thoroughly altered the original composition of flora and fauna. Extensive, uniform commercial cultivation has eliminated vast sections of native grassland where large animals such as pronghorns and elk formerly roamed. Perhaps the greatest changes in the bird population have been the result of alteration of water resources. Channeling and damming of rivers, irrigation, construction of artificial lakes and reservoirs, and unregulated development and urbanization, along with a host of other changes, have caused population explosions of some species. For example, starlings, cowbirds, Cliff Swallows, and blackbirds have thrived while more specialized birds such as Yellow-billed Cuckoos and Willow Flycatchers, which were once common in formerly widespread riparian habitats, are especially threatened by these alterations. Savannas—grasslands with scattered trees such as oaks—have suffered greatly from overgrazing. Once-beautiful areas of rolling hills dotted with native trees and vegetation have been converted to sterile, bare rangeland or unsightly development.

Species of small migrants (warblers, vireos, flycatchers) and larger birds (Cattle Egrets, mockingbirds, orioles) are attracted by new sources of water to orchards and other exotic plantings. There are also a number of wildlife refuges harboring great numbers of birds, especially waterfowl, in the winter. These areas, in combination with remnants of native habitats, always make birding in this valley challenging and interesting. This chapter also includes the lower-elevation foothills bordering the Central Valley and covers such habitats as chaparral, arid canyons, and deciduous woodlands up to the montane coniferous forests.

Wildlife refuge, Glenn County

Turkey Vulture
Cathartes aura 27", wingspread 69"

Turkey Vultures, also called buzzards, derive their name from the naked red skin of the adults' heads; the immatures' heads are dark. Vultures feed almost exclusively on decaying animal carcasses and other refuse, which they locate with sharp eyesight and a keen sense of smell—they are one of the few bird species possessing the latter sense. Constantly searching for food, they soar for miles, often high in the sky, with large flocks frequently congregating over a find. Their six-foot outstretched wings have a conspicuous two-toned appearance below, with the forward half darker and trailing part lighter. Vultures do not build nests—they lay their eggs on sheltered cliffs, in hollow trees, or even on the ground.

Northern Harrier
Circus cyaneus 20", wingspread 43"

Formerly called Marsh Hawk, harriers course back and forth low over the ground when hunting for rodents, snakes, small birds, and frogs. Conspicuous white rumps and relatively narrow, long wings identify these hawks of marshes and fields. Females are larger than males and are brown rather than gray. Nests are commonly built on the ground in tall weeds or reeds, or on top of a low bush above water. Adults will utter various shrill screams and dive on predators or anyone approaching too closely to nesting sites. These hawks are more common in California in winter, as individuals that nest in northern regions move south, especially during severe weather.

Red-shouldered Hawk
Buteo lineatus 19", wingspread 40"

This hawk's name is derived from its reddish wing coverts, or "shoulders," which sometimes are difficult to see. The flight is distinctive, with several quick wing beats and a glide, usually low over treetops. Red-shouldered Hawks prefer moist, mixed woodlands, and in some areas it is not unusual to see 5 to 10 individuals per day, often sitting on power lines. Adults are a rich reddish color below; at one time these birds were called Red-bellied Hawks. Nests are well built in the fork of a branch, 20 to 60 feet up and against the main tree trunk. They are often used for several years. Prey consists of snakes, frogs, mice, and sometimes small birds.

Turkey Vulture

Northern Harrier, female

Red-shouldered Hawk, immature

Red-tailed Hawk   *Buteo jamaicensis* 22", wingspread 50"

These are common large hawks frequently seen soaring slowly overhead in a wide variety of habitats, ranging from mountains and woodlands to fields and even residential areas. They like to perch in trees and the tops of poles along roadways. Plumage is variable, with combinations of dark and light patterns on their underparts; only adults have red tails. They prey on rodents, rabbits, frogs, snakes, lizards, and occasionally feed on carrion. Unfortunately, these beautiful hawks are an easy target and are frequently shot, even though they are fully protected by state and federal law. Nests are large and bulky, built high in a tree or on a cliff face. Red-tails have a distinctive call, a loud, harsh, descending *kree-e-e*.

California Quail   *Callipepla californica* 10"

California Quail frequent chaparral, brushy fields, open woodlands, farms, and suburban residential areas. Females lack the male's black face, their plumage is duller, and they have shorter head plumes (see the photograph on the back cover). These birds are ground nesters, and broods are large. Young are precocious and though able to walk and feed themselves almost immediately after hatching are vulnerable to predators, especially cats. Quail scratch like chickens for seeds, berries, and insects, and are easily attracted to feeders. Their call is a single note or a three-syllabled *chi-ca-go*. The California Quail is our state bird.

Red-tailed Hawk, perched

Red-tailed Hawk in flight

California Quail, male

Sandhill Crane
Grus canadensis 41"

Cranes fly with their necks outstretched and should not be confused with herons and egrets, which fly with necks folded back. These stately birds nest in Alaska, northern Canada, and into northeastern California. Immature cranes are basically brown with no red on their crowns and take about three years to attain adult plumage. Sandhill Cranes mate for life, and in early spring pairs perform a dramatic, graceful courtship dance, with both birds leaping high into the air and bowing before each other. Some individuals may perform this dance in any season, with immatures occasionally joining in. Nests are placed on a mound of marsh plants in shallow water or on the ground and may be up to five feet across. Two spotted, greenish eggs are laid. Feeding in summer is mostly in or near the breeding marshes, but in winter these birds gather in huge flocks and consume roots, grain, berries, rodents, small birds, insects, and snakes in large, dry fields. At night, they usually retire to the middle of a large, shallow lake for protection from predators.

Western Screech-Owl
Otus kennicottii 8½"

These small owls are residents of low-elevation open oak and riparian woodlands and suburban areas but are not easily observed because they are strictly nocturnal. Apparent ears are only feather tufts, which they often flatten flush on their heads. Screech-owls build nests in natural tree cavities or in old woodpecker holes. They feed on rodents, insects, and small birds. Their call is a descending series of notes that starts slowly and accelerates slightly toward the end.

Mountain Plover
Charadrius montanus 9"

Plovers are considered shorebirds, but this species is a bird of dry plains, grasslands, and plowed fields. Mountain Plovers nest on high plateaus in the Rocky Mountain and Plains states. They are observed in California only in winter, mostly on the west side of the Central Valley. They gather in flocks, feeding on insects gleaned from the ground. These plovers are often overlooked because of their protective coloration. When approached closely, they either run away or fly low, usually only a short distance, before alighting again.

36

Sandhill Cranes, pair with chicks

Western Screech-Owl

Mountain Plover, winter

Great Horned Owl
Bubo virginianus 22"

Great Horned Owls are California's largest owls and are resident in woodlands, parks, and suburbs. The "horns" are really feather tufts. In the evening (and often all night), these owls are heard giving their calls, a series of deep, hooted notes at measured intervals. They nest early in the year, utilizing the large old nests of herons, hawks, or crows or building a new structure in a protected cliff niche or occasionally on the ground. Great Horned Owls are aggressive and will not hesitate to attack any intruder approaching their nesting sites. Their prey includes rabbits, insects, rats, snakes, and sometimes other owls.

Acorn Woodpecker
Melanerpes formicivorus 9"

Males closely resemble females but lack the black band between the white forehead and red crown. These woodpeckers are appropriately named because their primary habitat is in woodlands wherever there are oaks. They have a unique habit of storing acorns in small holes that they drill into tree bark and wooden utility poles. In addition to acorns, they feed on insects, fruit, and tree sap. In flight, their white rump and wing patches are distinctive. Acorn Woodpeckers live year-round in noisy, close-knit groups, frequently emitting loud, parrotlike calls.

Nuttall's Woodpecker
Picoides nuttallii 7½"

Like many woodpecker species, only adult male Nuttall's have red on the back of the crown. This is a common woodpecker of streamside woodlands and oak forests below 6,000 feet. Woodpeckers have thick-walled skulls with strong skull and jaw muscles, which enable them to absorb the shock of pounding. Their long, wormlike tongues have barbed tips for extracting insects from holes. Males frequently drum loudly on resonant tree limbs or utility poles to establish territories. Nesting holes are drilled at varying heights in trees, and an average of five white eggs are laid.

Great Horned Owl

Acorn Woodpecker, female

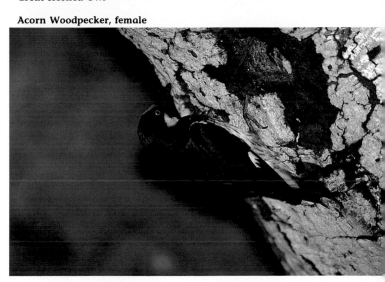

Nuttall's Woodpecker, male

Downy Woodpecker
Picoides pubescens 6¾"

Male Downy Woodpeckers have the red patch on the nape that is usual in male woodpeckers but lacking in females. This is the smallest of California's woodpeckers, similar to Nuttall's Woodpecker except for the large white patch on the Downy's back. Habitats include riparian woodlands and parks. There is some movement to higher elevations in late summer. Woodpeckers excavate new holes every nesting season, while previous years' sites are often used by birds such as bluebirds and chickadees. In the fall, both sexes dig fresh holes in dead tree stubs for winter roosting sites. Their calls include a sharp *pik* and a rapid series of high-pitched notes running down the scale.

Horned Lark
Eremophila alpestris 7¼"

The Horned Lark is one of California's most abundant birds, especially in winter. The apparent "horns," actually feather tufts, are more conspicuous in males. Nests are built on the ground, usually near grass clumps or earth clods. After nesting, larks gather in flocks sometimes numbering in the hundreds and move across bare fields, feeding on insects, weed seeds, and waste grain. This species walks or runs; most other birds hop. Males perform elaborate courtship displays, including flying and circling at considerable heights, while voicing high-pitched, tinkling songs.

Western Kingbird
Tyrannus verticalis 8¾"

Western Kingbirds are common summer residents of open country with scattered trees. They perch conspicuously on wires, trees, fences, or utility poles. In typical flycatcher fashion, they dart out from perches to snap up flying insects and then return to the beginning point. Nests are usually constructed high in trees or sometimes on buildings. These birds will attack hawks, crows, ravens, or any other potential predator without hesitation. Their winter range is chiefly from Mexico to Costa Rica. On their return to California, kingbirds are one of the harbingers of springtime.

Downy Woodpecker, female

Horned Lark, male

Western Kingbird

Tree Swallow
Tachycineta bicolor 5¾"

Tree Swallows are the swallows most likely to be seen in winter, and in summer they are common in any wooded habitat near water where abundant dead trees provide nesting cavities. They will also utilize holes in fence posts, the eaves of buildings, and some-times nest boxes. Both males and females can show either iridescent blue or green on the back, while immatures have brown upperparts. Some males may have two mates at the same time in the same season. This species generally migrates north earlier in the spring (as early as January) than other swallows and lingers longer in fall when flocks, sometimes numbering in the thousands, move south.

Northern Rough-winged Swallow *Stelgidopteryx serripennis* 5½"

This swallow derives its name from small curved hooks along the outermost feather of each wing, observable when the bird is exam-ined in hand. This is the more common of the two brown-backed swallows seen in California. Most small birds are night migrants, but swallows travel by day, coursing low over fields and water systems, catching insects (their exclusive food) on the wing. This species usually nests in burrows they dig in banks near water, but sometimes holes in structures or old ground squirrel holes are utilized. Rough-wings tend to be more solitary than other swallows, but several pairs may build nests close together in small colonies, sometimes mixed in with other swallow species.

Cliff Swallow
Hirundo pyrrhonota 5½"

According to legend, Cliff Swallows arrive in the spring at the mission in San Juan Capistrano and depart in the fall on exactly the same dates every year. This swallow winters in South America, moving north in the spring on a fairly precise schedule but not as exact as is claimed. Arrival at any certain location can vary as much as a week either way, depending on weather and food supply. Gourd-shaped mud nests are built, often by the hundreds, under bridges or building eaves or on cliff faces and even tree trunks. Some males may have two mates in the same season and mate with different females each year. Cliff Swallows are early migrants, moving along together with other swallow species, sometimes in large numbers. The song is a sweet, liquid chatter given when flying or from a perch near the nest.

Tree Swallow

Northern Rough-winged Swallow

Cliff Swallows, gathering mud for nests

Barn Swallow
Hirundo rustica 6¾"

The Barn Swallow, perhaps the most beautiful and graceful of all California's swallows, is our only swallow with a deeply forked tail. Females look much like males but have duller plumage overall. Barn Swallows migrate from Alaska to Argentina, possibly the longest route of any North American land bird. Nesting can be either in colonies or singly. Nests are mud cups mixed with straw or dried grass and lined with feathers and placed in natural cavities of dirt banks, on farm outbuildings, in caves, or under bridges. These swallows, like all others, are strictly insect eaters and will even follow a plowing farmer to catch stirred-up prey.

Yellow-billed Magpie
Pica nuttalli 16½"

Yellow-billed Magpies are endemic (unique) to California. They are restricted to the Sacramento and San Joaquin Valleys and the interior Coast Ranges from San Francisco to Santa Barbara in oak canyons and valleys of the coastal mountains. Magpies are closely related to crows and jays and, like them, are usually wary of people under natural conditions. They can become tame when not molested and are attracted to regular feeding by people. Their normal diet consists of insects augmented by acorns, carrion, grain, and berries. Nests are built in the crowns of tall trees, far out on small limbs and in loose colonies. The nest itself is a bulky, covered cradle of twigs with two entrances. Magpies are year-round residents, with some local movement after nesting.

Bushtit
Psaltriparus minimus 4½"

Females have pale eyes, males dark eyes. Most of the year, these tiny birds travel in flocks as they forage through trees and bushes for insects, their principal food. They do not have a song, but make their presence known by a chorus of soft chipping notes. Pairs begin to separate from flocks early in the spring (March) to nest, and often two broods are raised in a season. Nests are long, intricately woven, concealed pendants of plant fibers, suspended from tree or bush branches and with an entrance hole near the top.

Barn Swallow, male

Yellow-billed Magpie

Bushtit, male

Bewick's Wren
Thryomanes bewickii 5¼"

The name is pronounced the same as the automobile's, Buick. Long white eyebrows and a comparatively long tail identify these common wrens of brushlands, bushy stream edges, and open woods. Food consists primarily of insects, and nesting sites include almost any kind of cavity, both natural and man-made. Nests are made of moss, sticks, or dead leaves and lined with feathers. Five to seven white, irregularly spotted eggs are laid. Songs are variable, most beginning with several slurred notes followed by a trill.

Ruby-crowned Kinglet
Regulus calendula 4¼"

Kinglets are active, nervous birds, constantly flicking their wings rapidly. The male's red crown patch is seldom visible except when he becomes excited. These tiny birds nest in montane coniferous forests and descend to lowland thickets and wooded areas in wintertime. During migration and on wintering grounds, they are seen singly or in small, loose groups with other birds such as warblers, titmice, and nuthatches. Food primarily consists of insects along with some fruit, spiders, and tree sap. Kinglets are sometimes attracted to gardens by peanut butter and hummingbird feeders.

Western Bluebird
Sialia mexicana 7"

Females have duller plumage overall than males, and young birds have spotted breasts, which are characteristic of the thrush family. These birds are common in open woodlands at lower elevations and mountain forest edges below 5,000 feet. Nests are built in natural tree cavities or old woodpecker holes, and five blue eggs comprise the usual clutch. Food is mostly insects along with spiders and berries. In winter, there is some movement to lower altitudes and latitudes.

Bewick's Wren

Ruby-crowned Kinglet, male

Western Bluebird, male

Hermit Thrush

Catharus guttatus 6¾"

This thrush has a distinctive reddish brown tail, which it often quickly lifts and then slowly lowers. In California, it breeds in the mountains and coastal coniferous forests, moving to Mexico and Central America in the fall. Nests are usually built on the ground in a natural depression or low in a small tree. Many individuals migrate from farther north and winter in northern California. These solitary birds feed low in bushes or by foraging on the ground for insects and berries. Most members of the thrush family are excellent songsters, and Hermit Thrushes are among the finest with their ascending and descending clear, flutelike notes.

California Thrasher

Toxostoma redivivum 12"

Thrashers are closely related to mockingbirds and have similar habits and songs. This bird is a resident of chaparral, dense brush with scattered trees, and streamside thickets. Their long, curved bills are used to rummage amid leaf litter and probe the ground for grubs, spiders, and seeds. They will regularly come to bird feeders. Nests are made of twigs and grass and are built deep in thick shrubbery, low to the ground. This species is the only thrasher likely to be encountered in western and central California. They do not migrate, although there is some local movement in winter.

Wrentit

Chamaea fasciata 6½"

The habitat of this bird is exclusively thick brush and chaparral. It is normally a shy bird, staying deep in dense shrubbery, but at times it will come out and be amazingly tame. Although not a member of the wren family, Wrentits act much like wrens with their frequent tail cocking and feeding habits. These birds have a loud, ringing song consisting of three or four sharp notes followed by a metallic trill somewhat resembling a bouncing ping-pong ball. Their normal diet mostly consists of insects and berries, but they will eat a variety of other foods put out at feeding stations. Pairs mate for life and keep to fairly small, restricted territories.

Hermit Thrush

California Thrasher

Wrentit

American Pipit
Anthus rubescens 6½"

Pipits rarely nest in California, and then only high in the treeless mountain tundra, but large numbers winter throughout the state in lowland fields, wet meadows, and on ocean beaches. They bob their tails when walking and do not hop like other species. Their white outer tail feathers are conspicuous only in flight. They feed on insects and seeds, sometimes in large flocks. Call notes, frequently uttered, are two-syllabled and sound like *pi-pit* or *tsee-tseet*. This species was formerly called Water Pipit.

Phainopepla
Phainopepla nitens 7¾"

Males are black with conspicuous white wing patches; females are gray with pale wing patches. Food is principally mistletoe and other berries, along with insects. Breeding habitats are lowland oak savannas and wooded foothills. Phainopeplas spread mistletoe when they excrete the sticky seeds, and many mistletoe clusters mark the sites of former nests. Nests are small, neat cups of fine plant fibers placed in the fork of a limb 6 to 15 feet above ground. Clutches consist of two or three light green eggs covered with fine spots.

Loggerhead Shrike
Lanius ludovicianus 9"

Shrikes superficially resemble mockingbirds with their similar colors and patterns but have thick hooked bills and black masks. These are birds of open country with scattered trees and brush. Shrikes will sit on conspicuous perches or wires and pounce on insects, lizards, mice, and occasionally small birds. They often impale their prey on a sharp twig, thorn, or barbed-wire fence for later consumption. Sometimes these larders are raided by other birds such as mockingbirds. Nests are built deep in a thick bush or tree and are made of twigs and lined with fine material. About five white eggs with dark spots are laid, and two broods a season are common. In recent years, numbers of Loggerhead Shrikes have declined throughout most of their range.

American Pipit, winter

Phainopepla, male

Loggerhead Shrike

Orange-crowned Warbler   *Vermivora celata* 5"

The orange crown is usually concealed by greenish head feathers. These are active little birds, constantly searching for insects on low tree limbs and in brush. Breeding areas in California are along the coast and in mountain foothills in willow thickets, oak woodlands, and tall chaparral. Nests are built on the ground at the bases of bushes or low in shrubs. Orange-crowns are common migrants throughout northern California, with many spending the winter at lower elevations. Their song, frequently heard in early spring, is a high-pitched, even trill. A common note is a sharp, metallic *chip*.

Yellow-rumped Warbler   *Dendroica coronata* 5½"

This warbler's yellow rump patch is conspicuous, especially when flying away from the observer, at all seasons and in all plumages. The boreal and eastern race of this species, formerly called Myrtle Warbler, regularly appears in northern California during the nonbreeding season. It shares the distinctive yellow rump patch of the western form, Audubon's Warbler, but has a white eyebrow instead of an eye ring and a white throat instead of yellow. Both races now are considered one species. Abundant winter residents throughout the lower elevations of northern California, Audubon's Warblers nest locally in the northern coastal district and commonly in the mountains but are absent elsewhere during summer. Many males attain their breeding plumage and begin to sing early in the spring while still on their wintering grounds. Females, fall immatures, and nonbreeding males of both races look basically like the fall female Myrtle Warbler pictured, except for the differences noted. On warm days, these small birds actively fly out from trees and bushes to catch insects in air.

Orange-crowned Warbler

Yellow-rumped Warbler, spring Audubon male

Yellow-rumped Warbler, fall Myrtle female

Townsend's Warbler
Dendroica townsendi 5"

Warblers, with their bright colors and sprightly movements, are the butterflies of the bird world. Adult male Townsend's have large black patches on their throats. Females and immatures look much like males but are duller and paler. This bird nests in the towering northwestern coniferous forests north of California and forages in the treetops for weevils, insects, and caterpillars. A common migrant, these warblers can be found in all kinds of habitats during their southerly and northerly movements. Although the winter range of this species extends south to Nicaragua, many spend the season in the forests of the Coast Ranges of northern California.

Wilson's Warbler
Wilsonia pusilla 4¾"

Some immatures and adult females lack the male's distinctive black cap. This little warbler prefers to actively glean insects close to or on the ground, not high in trees as most of its relatives do. Wilson's Warblers are common migrants throughout the lowlands. They breed in the mountains and coastal forests, where they nest on the ground or low in bushes near streams or other moist areas. Numbers of individuals nesting at lower elevations have been reduced because of cowbird parasitism. Wintering grounds are in Mexico and Central America.

Black-headed Grosbeak
Pheucticus melanocephalus 8¼"

The brown females and young have striped heads with streaks above and below. The large bill is used to split open hard seeds and nuts. Other food includes insects, berries, and fruit. Grosbeaks nest in open woodlands, usually near water. Males arrive at breeding grounds about a week before the females, but only females build nests, which are loosely constructed of twigs and placed anywhere from low in bushes to high in trees. Both females and males aggressively defend their territories from intruding grosbeaks. Winter is spent in Mexico and Central America.

Townsend's Warbler, male

Wilson's Warbler, male

Black-headed Grosbeak, male

Lazuli Bunting
Passerina amoena 5½"

Brownish females and immatures have just a tinge of blue in the wings and tail. It takes two years for the male to attain his brilliant blue breeding plumage. When wintering in Mexico, males have femalelike plumage, which gradually turns blue as they migrate northward. These buntings nest at elevations ranging from near sea level at the humid coast to about 5,000 feet in the Sierra Nevada. Habitat is mixed woodlands and thickets, usually near water. Food is primarily insects and seeds. Males proclaim territories by singing a bright, rapid song of high-pitched, varied notes from treetops, wires, or tops of tall bushes.

Rufous-sided Towhee
Pipilo erythrophthalmus 8½"

This is a bird of dense, shrubby habitats throughout California. It feeds on the ground, busily scratching the earth and leaf litter with its long claws for insects, seeds, and berries. Females look much like males but have slightly duller plumage overall and slaty brown rather than black hoods. Towhees winter over much of their nesting range, with some withdrawal from higher elevations. Well-concealed nests are built by females on the ground or in low bushes. Although fairly shy, these birds will come to seed feeders. The song is a buzzy trill, and the call note is a sharp *wank*.

Savannah Sparrow
Passerculus sandwichensis 5½"

Sparrows are among the most difficult birds to identify. Many species look alike, with variation within individual species adding to the confusion. Most are residents of grasslands and marshes, where they're often hard to see well because of their habit of flying away erratically, then dropping to the ground and running quickly through dense vegetation. In winter, California is home to many races of Savannah Sparrows, with the one pictured being the most common and widespread. During the nesting season, males will perch on tall bushes or grass and sing a thin, buzzy trill of varying pitch. Nests are built on the ground, well concealed in grass tussocks.

Lazuli Bunting, male

Rufous-sided Towhee, male

Savannah Sparrow

Western Meadowlark
Sturnella neglecta 9½"

Meadowlarks are birds of grasslands, cultivated fields, and pastures at lower elevations and on occasion can be found in mountain meadows. When walking or perched they frequently flick open their tails, showing prominent white outer tail feathers. Nests are well hidden on the ground in grass clumps, domed with an entrance on the side; five white, speckled eggs are laid. Males defend their territories by singing loudly from tall weeds, posts, bushes, and even in flight. Meadowlarks fly with quick wing flaps between short glides. After the breeding season, they gather in flocks together with northern birds that have moved south for the winter.

Brown-headed Cowbird
Molothrus ater 7½"

This species does not build a nest of its own, but the uniformly grayish brown female will lay a single egg in up to 12 different nests of other small bird species. After hatching, the young cowbird grows rapidly by seizing all the food brought in by the unsuspecting host birds, eventually starving or pushing the original nestlings out of the nest. With increased agricultural production and fragmentation of natural habitats the cowbird population has grown greatly, putting tremendous pressure on many species of small songbirds. After the breeding season, adult and young cowbirds gather in large flocks, often with other species of blackbirds.

American Goldfinch
Carduelis tristis 5"

This bird is often called "wild canary." Females and immatures lack the black cap and are olive-brown above and olive-yellow below. Winter males resemble the females. These are birds of open woodlands and riparian habitats. In fall and winter they gather in flocks and feed on all kinds of seeds in weedy fields, gardens, and brush. Nests are small, neat cups built in a fork of a tree or shrub. All three species of goldfinches found in California (American, Lesser, and Lawrence's) have similar appearances and habits. Goldfinches bound through the air with a characteristic undulating flight. The song is a lively, high-pitched series of trills and twitters frequently given while flying.

Western Meadowlark

Brown-headed Cowbirds, female and male

American Goldfinch, breeding male

Here are additional birds, described elsewhere in this book, that frequently appear in the Central Valley. Most of the birds referred to in Chapter V, Birds of Freshwater Wetlands and Riparian Woodlands, can also be observed in suitable habitats in the Central Valley.

Species	*Preferred Locality*
California Gull	flooded fields
Ring-billed Gull	flooded fields
Barn Owl	farm buildings
Mourning Dove	open country
Anna's Hummingbird	flowers
Northern Flicker	suburbs and savannas
Scrub Jay	shrubland with scattered trees
Common Crow	scattered trees
Say's Phoebe	open country
White-breasted Nuthatch	wooded areas
Plain Titmouse	wooded areas
House Wren	wooded areas
American Robin	open country and woods
Northern Mockingbird	brushy areas, towns and cities
Yellow-rumped Warbler	everywhere in winter
European Starling	open country and farmlands
House Sparrow	near human habitations
Red-winged Blackbird	with other blackbirds
Brewer's Blackbird	moist cultivated areas
House Finch	brush near buildings

Sierra Nevada,
Mariposa County,
Yosemite National Park

Coastal redwood forest, Humboldt County

Chapter III
Birds of the Mountains
and Lowland Coniferous Forests

Evergreen (coniferous or boreal) forests cover the slopes of California's high mountains. In the Sierra Nevada they begin above 4,000 feet on the western slope and at about 7,000 feet on the eastern escarpment. Similar forests with some of the same bird species are found in other mountains like the Cascades and coastal ranges and extend down to the seashore.

The Sierra Nevada is a huge mountain chain more than 430 miles long and about 80 miles wide running approximately north and south down the eastern one-third of California. Because of its elevation (many peaks rise more than 14,000 feet) and extremes of temperature and precipitation, this mountain range contains a great variety of complex habitats in close proximity and interspersed with one another. Several rivers bordered by riparian forests drain westward into the Central Valley. Dense forests of pine, cedar, and fir range up to timberline (about 10,500 feet), above which there is a paucity of birdlife because of frigid winters with high winds and deep snow, short summers, and scanty vegetation and cover. Scattered within the major habitats are other ecological niches such as tundra, lakes, wet meadows, sheltered valleys, and several types of forests, such as giant sequoia, red fir, lodgepole pine, aspen, and oak.

The Coast Ranges are low, intermittent mountain systems running primarily north and south. They are forested mainly with Douglas fir, coast redwoods, chaparral (a low, thick-leaved, twiggy, usually dense forest), pines, and oaks. These forests are nurtured by coastal fog and rain and are not subject to the climatic extremes typical of higher mountains.

Other major ranges included in this chapter are the Klamath, Cascade, White, and Warner Mountains, plus a number of smaller chains. Many birds are common to various highland areas throughout California. Feeding stations, once established, especially in the higher elevations, should be maintained throughout the year to avoid endangering birds that have become dependent on this food source when sudden shifts in weather occur.

Coastal evergreen forests range from the magnificent redwoods in the northwest to a mix of Douglas fir, bay, madrone, and other tree types in the south. Below Monterey, as annual rainfall diminishes, the tree types gradually change to mostly deciduous forms, although large sections of coniferous forests can be found where supported by required local precipitation. Several kinds of birds typical of mountainous areas are regular residents, with additional species joining them from the highlands and regions farther north during migration and in winter. Among birds found in both highland and lowland evergreen forests are Steller's Jays, American Robins, Dark-eyed Juncos, and Chipping Sparrows.

Mountain coniferous and riparian habitats, Lassen County

Mountain Quail
Oreortyx pictus 11"

Female Mountain Quail are similar in plumage and pattern to males but have shorter head plumes. Habitat is generally montane chaparral and brushy mountain forests. Quail eat a variety of food including buds, insects, seeds, and berries. The nest is a leaf-lined depression on the ground usually at the base of a bush, log, or rock, and often more than a dozen buff-colored eggs are laid. After nesting, family groups frequently gather in large flocks and move to lower elevations almost entirely on foot.

Northern Saw-whet Owl
Aegolius acadicus 8"

Saw-whet Owls are strictly nocturnal, but they can be approached closely if surprised during the day. Because of their retiring habits, the distribution and seasonal status of these owls in California are poorly understood. The name is derived from its raspy call, which sounds like a saw being sharpened. Its primary vocalization, however, is a long series of *toot* notes, whistled at about two-second intervals. Saw-whet Owls nest at mid- and lower elevations, and in some winters local numbers are greatly increased by major invasions of birds from the north. Nests are made in old woodpecker holes or natural cavities. The usual diet is mainly insects, sometimes augmented by small rodents and birds.

Band-tailed Pigeon
Columba fasciata 14½"

Although these pigeons superficially resemble the introduced Rock Doves that are abundant in lowland urban areas, this is a native species whose primary habitat is midelevation oak and coniferous forests. Nests are made of sticks and flimsily constructed far out on a horizontal limb. Unlike most members of its family, Band-tailed Pigeons lay only one instead of two white eggs, and often two broods a season are raised using the same nest. During fall and winter, these pigeons wander irregularly in search of acorns, pine and fir nuts, and grain and berries, with numbers of birds fluctuating greatly at any given locality.

Mountain Quail, male   Northern Saw-whet Owl

Band-tailed Pigeon

Common Nighthawk

Chordeiles minor 9½"

Nighthawks are slender, graceful fliers seen at dusk hunting for aerial insects. They are members of the nightjar family and are not hawks. Even though they are usually seen and heard only at night in most areas, individuals can often be found during daytime, roosting on the ground or on fence posts. East of the Sierra-Cascade mountain ranges, it's not unusual to find nighthawks feeding, flying, and calling during the day. These birds breed in the northern part of the state and locally in the Sierra Nevada. Females lack the white throat and white in the tail. Their call, heard from high in the sky, is a nasal *peent*. Two speckled eggs are laid, usually on the bare ground and sometimes on flat roofs or stumps. Winter is spent in South America.

Red-breasted Sapsucker

Sphyrapicus ruber 8½"

A member of the woodpecker family, Red-breasted Sapsuckers nest in coniferous and mixed coniferous-deciduous forests of mountain ranges. Sapsuckers drill small horizontal rows in tree bark, feeding on sap and insects attracted to the sap. Possibly, as some people claim, these birds damage fruit trees with their drilling. Nests are excavated in live deciduous trees near water or in big conifers, including giant sequoias, and are lined with wood chips. Several nesting holes may be started before a final one is chosen. There is some downslope and southerly movement after the nesting season.

Allen's Hummingbird

Selasphorus sasin 3¾"

Allen's males are very similar to male Rufous Hummingbirds but have green instead of orange backs. The females and immature males of both species have speckled throats, green backs and tails, and a pale cinnamon wash on the flanks, making it difficult to separate the two species in these plumages. Allen's Hummingbirds are residents of the humid coastal belt and are early nesters, sometimes beginning in February. They often raise two broods in one season. Nests are well built even for a hummingbird and are made of plant down, flower blossoms, leaves, and spider webs, decorated on the outside with lichen and lined with feathers on the interior. Most of the population winters in northwestern Mexico, but a few remain all year in coastal southern California.

Common Nighthawk, male

Red-breasted Sapsucker

Allen's Hummingbird, male

White-headed Woodpecker
Picoides albolarvatus 9¼"

This distinctive woodpecker is a year-round resident of California's mountain pine forests and is the only North American woodpecker with a white head. The head, combined with conspicuous white wing patches in flight, makes this species readily identifiable. White-headed Woodpeckers often alight on trunks or branches upside down or sidewise. In addition to its nesting hole, sometimes several other holes are excavated in the same stump. It consumes large quantities of pine-cone seeds and forages on loose tree bark for insects and spiders.

Black-backed Woodpecker
Picoides arcticus 9½"

Most woodpeckers have four toes on each foot, but this one has only three, two forward and one back. An uncommon species, it inhabits higher-elevation coniferous forests and is often found in burned-over areas. Black-backed Woodpeckers forage on dead conifers in search of larvae and insects, flaking away large patches of loose bark rather than drilling. Seasonally, they will also feed on fruit and come to the ground for acorns. The female lacks the yellow cap. Nests are cavities in live lodgepole pines and dead stubs and trunks, with entrance holes beveled at the lower edge.

Pileated Woodpecker
Dryocopus pileatus 16½"

Almost crow size, Pileated Woodpeckers are the largest woodpeckers still found in North America. Females have less red on their heads and lack the red mustache. Both sexes drum loudly, but females less often and at lower volume than males. Pairs will occupy the same territory year after year, with each bird digging and using one of several roosting cavities. Nesting holes are large and oval or rectangular shaped. This woodpecker tears off big pieces of wood and strips of bark to get to wood-boring beetles. These are uncommon birds, restricted to mixed conifers and hardwood forests in the Sierra Nevada and coastal ranges, south to Santa Cruz County.

White-headed Woodpecker, male

Black-backed Woodpecker, male

Pileated Woodpecker, male

Olive-sided Flycatcher *Contopus borealis* 7½"

This flycatcher habitually perches on the tip-top of a tall tree giving its distinctive, clear song, *hick-three-beers*. The dark sides and flanks, along with the sometimes visible white tufts on the sides of the rump, help distinguish this bird from similar-looking species. It's fairly common, though declining, in open coniferous forests and eucalyptus groves from lowlands to high in mountains. Nests are built far out on horizontal limbs in clusters of twigs, with the usual clutch consisting of three pale, brown-spotted eggs. Olive-sided Flycatchers winter in South America.

Western Wood-Pewee *Contopus sordidulus* 6¼"

Western Wood-Pewees are grayish brown flycatchers found throughout the wooded areas of California. This common but often overlooked bird has the usual flycatcher habit of darting out, catching a flying insect, and returning to the original perch. Its nest, made of grassy materials, is covered with lichen and placed on a horizontal tree limb. A regular call is a harsh one- or two-noted slurred buzz sounding like *peeer*. It is present in California from late April to September; its winter range is from Mexico to South America.

Hammond's Flycatcher *Empidonax hammondii* 5½"

Like several similar-looking flycatchers encountered in California, which are difficult to identify even by experienced observers, this species' general appearance is that of an active, small, olive-colored flycatcher with two pale wing bars and a small, dark bill. Although a summer resident of high-mountain humid coniferous forests, it can be found during migration throughout the state in lower-elevation woodlands and thickets. Hammond's Flycatchers are rarely seen in winter; most travel to Mexico and Central America for the season.

Olive-sided Flycatcher

Western Wood-Pewee

Hammond's Flycatcher

Pacific-slope Flycatcher   *Empidonax difficilis* 5½"

One of the group of small flycatchers that all look alike, Pacific-slope Flycatchers are a little easier to identify than most of the rest because they have yellowish underparts and teardrop-shaped eye rings that the others lack. Nesting habitat is typically in dense, shaded forests or tall riparian vegetation. It often flicks its wings nervously while foraging at low to moderate heights within the canopy. The usual call is a high, rising *psee-eeet*. This species is a common summer resident of California, with a few overwintering but most individuals migrating to Mexico and Central America in winter. Pacific-slope Flycatchers were formerly called Western Flycatchers.

Violet-green Swallow   *Tachycineta thalassina* 5¼"

A common resident of open woodlands in lowlands and mountains, Violet-green Swallows are daytime migrants to and from Central America early in spring and again in fall, with a few wintering locally along the California coast. Distinctive white patches on either side of the rump help identify this bird. Females and young lack the males' lustrous plumage but have the same basic color and pattern. Nests are built in loose colonies using natural cavities, old woodpecker holes, and occasionally buildings.

Steller's Jay   *Cyanocitta stelleri* 11½"

This jay is often confused with the Blue Jay of eastern North America because of their similar crests and blue coloration. Steller's Jays usually inhabit mountain forests and coastal coniferous woodlands, but they will regularly come into residential areas where there are tall trees. They do not migrate, but there is some local movement depending on food supply and weather. They have generally the same nesting and feeding habits as other jays—they build bulky stick nests, usually in evergreen trees, and forage in treetops and on the ground for seeds, fruit, and insects. They are often bold and noisy except in the vicinity of their nests. Steller's Jays have a variety of calls ranging from a series of soft liquid gurgles to loud whistles and shrieks.

Pacific-slope Flycatcher   **Violet-green Swallow, male**

Steller's Jay

Clark's Nutcracker　　　　　*Nucifraga columbiana* 12"

Nutcrackers are members of the same family as crows and jays and have many of the characteristics of those birds. Large white patches in the wings and tail are evident when flying. These extremely curious birds are easily attracted to campgrounds and picnic areas, where they scavenge for handouts. Nutcrackers often travel in loud, noisy flocks and usually remain in the mountains, although they periodically invade lowland areas during food shortages in the higher elevations.

Mountain Chickadee　　　　　*Parus gambeli* 5¼"

Chickadees are friendly, curious little birds that are easily attracted to home feeders in the mountains and to scraps at picnic areas and campgrounds. They build nests in natural cavities or old woodpecker holes, and often two broods a year are raised. After breeding, chickadees frequently wander to lowland residential areas, open woodlands, and riparian thickets, where they will sometimes join other birds in loose feeding flocks, searching together for insects, spiders, and seeds. The most frequently heard call is a slurred *chick-adee-adee-adee*.

Chestnut-backed Chickadee　　　　　*Parus rufescens* 4¾"

Birds of this species in northwestern California have bright chestnut sides and flanks, while those on the central California coast show just a trace of chestnut below. Their habitat is mainly in dark, humid, coniferous coastal forests, and to a limited extent in broad-leaved woods near streams. They are also found in small numbers at lower elevations around Yosemite on the west slope of the Sierra Nevada. These active little birds often travel in loose association with creepers, kinglets, and nuthatches. Natural food consists of insects, spiders, and fruit pulp, but they can be attracted to feeders by birdseed and suet. Nests are placed in natural cavities or woodpecker holes, though at times a pair will dig its own site in a rotted tree.

Clark's Nutcracker

Mountain Chickadee

Chestnut-backed Chickadee

White-breasted Nuthatch *Sitta carolinensis* 5¾"

Nuthatches are as comfortable foraging for insects head down on tree trunks and limbs as head up. This species is found in a wider variety of habitats than other nuthatches and is common in deciduous lowland woodlands as well as coniferous forests at higher elevations. Females are somewhat paler than males. After the fall family breakup, each member of a pair will feed and roost alone throughout the winter but will stay within calling distance of each other. Their most frequent call is a low-pitched, repeated, nasal *yank*. Nuthatches will come to feeding stations for seeds and suet.

Brown Creeper *Certhia americana* 5¼"

Creepers are common but often hard to see because they are so well camouflaged. They typically feed on insects by climbing and spiraling up tree trunks, then flying to a lower spot on a nearby tree to repeat the process. Nests are hidden under loose strips of bark against trunks of dead trees. Their primary habitats are coniferous, mixed, or swampy forests, but after nesting individuals can be found in any woodland. Creepers are generally solitary, but in winter they sometimes travel with flocks of titmice and nuthatches.

Pygmy Nuthatch *Sitta pygmaea* 4¼"

These nuthatches are found in pine, Monterey cypress, and Douglas-fir forests, where they search in flocks of up to 100 birds for insects, spiders, and pine seeds on tree trunks and outermost twigs high in the canopy. They often dig their own nest holes in dead trees or fallen logs, but they will also use old woodpecker holes. Pygmy Nuthatches are the smallest of all North American nuthatches and have the unusual habit of roosting in groups at night in tree cavities. During winter, flocks drift noisily through the tops of pines, calling and twittering incessantly.

White-breasted Nuthatch, male   **Brown Creeper**

Pygmy Nuthatch

Winter Wren

Troglodytes troglodytes 4"

Our smallest wren is the most difficult to observe because of its retiring habits. It nests in thick brush within moist coniferous woods, especially along stream banks, but in winter it can be found in the brushy understory of any type of woodland. Males build up to four dummy nests in addition to the actual one constructed by the pair together. Food consists of insects, spiders, and some berries. Its song, loud for such a small bird, is a rapid series of melodious, high-pitched trills that reverberates through the dense forest. Although there are a number of North American wrens, this is the only species found in Europe, where it is known simply as the Wren.

Mountain Bluebird

Sialia currucoides 7¼"

Open forests bordering high mountain meadows or sagebrush plains are the breeding grounds of this bluebird. Males are a bright sky blue; females and young are dull gray-brown with a tinge of blue. After nesting, Mountain Bluebirds gather in loose flocks and move to open areas at lower elevations. They catch insects in flight like flycatchers, or by hovering low over the ground and dropping down on them. Nests are built in natural cavities, including old woodpecker holes, and crevices in buildings.

American Dipper

Cinclus mexicanus 7½"

This interesting bird has several adaptations enabling it to live in and close to rushing mountain streams. It has a large preen gland (10 times the size of any other songbird's) that provides oil to keep its feathers waterproof, a movable flap over its nostrils to keep out water, and a nictitating membrane (flap) to protect its eyes. Dippers can swim below the water surface to catch caddis-fly larvae and other aquatic insects. Females build bulky nests, about one foot in diameter with a side entrance, on rocky ledges, sometimes behind waterfalls. They do not migrate but will move to lower altitudes if streams freeze.

Winter Wren   Mountain Bluebird, male

American Dipper

Swainson's Thrush
Catharus ustulatus 7"

These fairly common but shy birds breed in moist woods, swamps, and thickets from the lowlands up into the mountains. Their loud, ringing song can be heard spiraling upward day or night. During migration they can be found in any wooded area. Like most thrushes, Swainson's gather insects, earthworms, seeds, and berries from the ground. Nests are built on horizontal branches close to tree trunks or on the ground in root tangles along stream banks. Their winter range is from Mexico to South America.

Varied Thrush
Ixoreus naevius 9½"

Varied Thrushes are perhaps the most beautiful of all North American thrushes. The female's plumage resembles that of the male, but the pattern has much less contrast. This bird is a ground feeder, searching for insects, seeds, and berries. Males ascend to the tops of tall trees and sing an eerie, drawn-out, buzzy whistle that fades away at the end, all the while remaining concealed in the foliage. These thrushes breed from northwestern California to Alaska. In winter, they migrate into California in numbers that fluctuate from year to year and can be found in various wooded habitats, especially dense, moist, lowland coniferous forests.

Solitary Vireo
Vireo solitarius 5½"

Vireos are plain-colored, inconspicuous birds of broad-leaved lowland woods. They search slowly and deliberately for insects, generally staying high in trees and shrubs. Like most songbirds vireos enjoy bathing, but instead of splashing about in a shallow pool they will dive from a perch into the water and then quickly fly up to a nearby twig to shake and preen. This species is widespread along the northwest coast of California in the breeding season, where it nests at low elevations. Solitary Vireos are absent in summer from the Central Valley, though some pass through there during migration. Most of these vireos winter south as far as Nicaragua, but a few remain in California all year.

Swainson's Thrush

Varied Thrush, male

Solitary Vireo

Hutton's Vireo
Vireo huttoni 5"

This bird is primarily a resident of coastal oak forests and humid deciduous-coniferous woodlands but is partially migratory and wanders into other habitats in winter. It feeds in typical vireo fashion, moving slowly and deliberately through the foliage of trees and shrubs searching for insects, spiders, and berries. The nest, which this tiny bird will defend by vigorously attacking most intruders, is a deep cup suspended from a forked twig well out at the end of a branch. Hutton's Vireos somewhat resemble small flycatchers and kinglets, so caution should be exercised in their identification.

Hermit Warbler
Dendroica occidentalis 5½"

The unmarked yellow cheeks are a distinctive characteristic of this warbler. Males have black chins, throats, and napes, areas that are paler in females. Fairly common birds that nest in the tall conifers of mountains and northern coastal ranges, Hermit Warblers can also be seen in any wooded area during migration. They feed by flitting along tree branches, sometimes hanging like chickadees as they forage for insects and spiders. Occasionally this warbler hybridizes with Townsend's Warblers. The wintering grounds are in Mexico and Central America, with a few wintering in California's coastal coniferous forests.

MacGillivray's Warbler
Oporornis tolmiei 5¼"

MacGillivray's Warblers tend to stay close to the ground in thick brush, where they forage for insects. Females are duller and lack the males' black bibs. These fairly common birds are often overlooked because of their retiring habits. Nests are built near the ground in dense, moist bushes of the mountains and coastal northwestern California. During migration, MacGillivray's Warblers pass through diverse habitats including deserts, lowland brush, and wooded areas. They winter in Mexico and Central America.

Hutton's Vireo

Hermit Warbler, male

MacGillivray's Warbler, male

Western Tanager
Piranga ludoviciana 7¼"

Although Western Tanagers are mainly birds of mixed mountain forests, during migration they can be found in a wide variety of habitats throughout the lowlands, often traveling in large flocks. Females and young are greenish above and have dull yellow underparts. In the fall, adult males lose most of the red on their head, regaining it in the spring. Tanagers feed mostly on fruit and insects, which sometimes are caught in flycatcher fashion. Their nests are built well out on tree limbs fairly high off the ground. The song is a series of burry notes rising and lowering in pitch. A common call is a two-syllabled *pri-tick*. Like many California birds, Western Tanagers winter in Mexico and Central America.

Green-tailed Towhee
Pipilo chlorurus 7¼"

This species nests in mountain chaparral interspersed with pines. Normally secretive, in spring males sing from exposed perches a loud series of clear notes followed by a coarse trill. When alarmed, towhees will run or skulk through brush with their tails raised, much like chipmunks. They scratch the earth with their long claws, searching for seeds, berries, and insects. Nests are built on or near the ground at the base of a bush. They lay four white eggs, heavily speckled with brown. A few Green-tailed Towhees winter in southern California, but most travel to Mexico.

Fox Sparrow
Passerella iliaca 7"

These are California's largest sparrows. Their feeding and nesting habits and songs are much like those of towhees. California is host to many races or "subspecies" of Fox Sparrows throughout the year, especially during migration and winter. Most have similar plumage patterns but are various shades of brown, gray, and rufous, sometimes with bill sizes ranging from petite to massive. The subspecies that breeds in the mountains migrates to Mexico for the winter, while races from other parts of North America spend the season in brushy lowland areas of California.

Western Tanager, male

Green-tailed Towhee

Fox Sparrow

Dark-eyed Junco
Junco hyemalis 6¼"

Most juncos withdraw to the lowlands after breeding in the mountains and on the northern coast. There are several subspecies that winter in California, but all appear essentially the same, with hoods of varying shades of gray and other minor differences. California's resident bird (formerly called Oregon Junco) nests in forest edges at higher elevations and in fall gathers in flocks with other members of the sparrow family and moves into lowland parks and residential areas. Females build the nest, usually placed on the ground in a cup-shaped depression, frequently near water. The song is a flat, metallic trill.

Gray-crowned Rosy-Finch
Leucosticte tephrocotis 6¼"

Rocky outcroppings and snowbanks above timberline are the breeding habitat of rosy-finches. These birds have several unusual characteristics: the males outnumber females by about six to one, forcing them to constantly defend their mates from other males; both sexes have throat pouches capable of carrying small tundra plant seeds during the nesting season; and their bills change from black during the breeding season to yellow with a black tip the rest of the year. In winter, rosy-finches gather in large flocks and descend to the lower slopes of the eastern Sierra Nevada, where they often come to seed feeders.

Purple Finch
Carpodacus purpureus 6"

Purple Finches nest in lower- and midelevation oak and mixed oak-conifer woodlands. Females closely resemble females of the other two California red finches—refer to the section on the House Finch in Chapter I and Cassin's Finch in this chapter for comparisons. Depending on food supplies, numbers of Purple Finches vary from year to year. Some wander to higher elevations after breeding, then descend, especially after heavy snowfall, to wooded lower elevations. The song is a fast, musical warble of moderate length, repeated numerous times and vocalized by adult males and immature males, which look like females.

Dark-eyed Junco, male

Gray-crowned Rosy-Finch

Purple Finch, male

Cassin's Finch

Carpodacus cassinii 6¼"

Of California's three red finches, Cassin's Finches are the most likely to be seen at higher elevations, although there is some seasonal altitudinal overlap among the three. These finches move downslope after nesting, with numbers at any one location varying from time to time. Females and immature males lack the bright color of adult males and are heavily streaked with brown overall. Cassin's Finches forage from treetops down to the ground for conifer seeds and buds. They also eat insects and berries and will come to feeding stations. Nests are built in large conifers, out at the end of limbs.

Pine Siskin

Carduelis pinus 5"

These wide-ranging birds appear in different habitats depending on weather and food supply. Females build nests in loose colonies, typically about halfway up in conifers or deciduous trees, well out from the trunk and concealed in needles or leaves. In fall and winter, siskins often gather in large flocks, moving about in search of seeds and catkins. Yellow patches in the wings and tail are evident in flight. Among their several vocalizations is a long, buzzy, ascending trill, sung from treetops.

Lesser Goldfinch

Carduelis psaltria 4½"

Females and nonbreeding males are greenish above and dull yellow below, but all have white wing patches that are conspicuous in flight. This is the most widespread and common of the California goldfinches. They are found throughout the year in dry, brushy fields, woodland borders, and residential areas. The most preferred natural foods are thistle and other weed seeds, but they are easily attracted to feeders and birdbaths. Nests are neat cups of soft materials, placed in forks of branches. Their canary-like song is often given while flying.

Cassin's Finches, male and female

Pine Siskin

Lesser Goldfinch, breeding male

Listed below are some birds, described in other chapters, that can frequently be found in mountains and lowland evergreen or coniferous forests.

Species	Preferred Locality
Turkey Vulture	circling over clearings
Red-tailed Hawk	open woodlands
Golden Eagle	high overhead
Mourning Dove	open woodlands and fields
Great Horned Owl	open woodlands
White-throated Swift	cliffs
Northern Flicker	open woodlands
Downy Woodpecker	lower-elevation woodlands
Common Raven	most habitats at any elevation
Bushtit	open woodlands
Bewick's Wren	lower-elevation woodlands
American Robin	open forest
Hermit Thrush	forests
Ruby-crowned Kinglet	woodlands
Orange-crowned Warbler	forests and bushes
Yellow-rumped Warbler	forests
Brewer's Blackbird	moist areas
Black-headed Grosbeak	open woodlands
Purple Finch	lower-elevation woodlands
Rufous-sided Towhee	scrub woodlands
White-crowned Sparrow	meadows and chaparral

Birds following boat, San Francisco County

Rocky shore, Mendocino County

Chapter IV
Birds of the Coast and Nearby Ocean

California is blessed with a scenic coastline and interesting offshore islands. Additionally, its seashore and beaches, brackish (a mixture of salt water and fresh water) lagoons, rocky headlands, bays, tidal estuaries, and salt marshes are home to a rich and varied avian fauna. Certain birds found in these habitats are among the world's greatest travelers, coming and going enormous distances from the far reaches of the Northern Hemisphere to the Southern as seasonal drive dictates.

Only that part of the ocean within sight of land is discussed here. The open ocean is a vast, complex ecosystem beyond the scope of this book. Most people will not encounter many specialized pelagic (ocean) birds except when they venture far out on the sea. However, some of these avian travelers do come close to shore at places like Monterey Bay. By going on one of the regularly scheduled birding boats, it is possible to observe a sample of this fascinating aspect of ornithology. Most ocean birds do not wander aimlessly over the world's seas but are driven by some of the same factors as land birds. Season, food, ocean currents, and weather dictate direction and scope of flight. Most of these birds have special adaptations enabling them to drink salt water, thus allowing them to spend long periods of time far at sea, coming to land only to nest.

The most obvious ocean birds are gulls, usually all called "seagulls" by inexperienced people. In reality, there are many kinds of gulls along the California coast, and with practice, most can be identified by species and even approximate age can be determined. There are various shorebirds, including sandpipers and plovers, many with only subtle differences in appearance that challenge the most knowledgeable observer. The young of large birds can be confused with fully grown individuals of different species. Shorebirds gather in vast numbers on tidal flats at low tide, feeding on rich and varied food sources in the exposed mud. Birds with different shaped and sized bills are so highly specialized that there is no direct competition for a particular food resource. Ducks, loons, and grebes are among many varieties of birds that can be found seasonally in abundance on lagoons and bays. Salt marshes, a fast-disappearing habitat due to development for marinas, housing, and other uses, attract a number of distinctive birds, some of which are on the verge of extinction because most of their habitat has been destroyed.

Several species discussed in Chapter V, Birds of Freshwater Wetlands and Riparian Woodlands, can also regularly be observed in similar localities along or near the coast, especially during migration.

Saltwater marsh, San Luis Obispo County

Pacific Loon
Gavia pacifica 26"

Of the three kinds of loons that commonly winter in California, the Pacific Loon is the species most likely to be seen out at sea. Winter plumages of each variety closely resemble one another, and all appear much like the immature Pacific Loon illustrated. Loons superficially resemble ducks but are larger, with long bodies and daggerlike bills. These birds swim or dive in search of fish, crustaceans, and other aquatic life. Pacific Loons nest from Alaska across northern Canada to Hudson Bay. In late-spring breeding plumage, most individuals show pale gray heads and napes, iridescent purple throats (appearing black in most lighting conditions), and black and white upperparts. Winter is spent mostly along the coast, with rare strays appearing inland in the fall.

Horned Grebe
Podiceps auritus 13½"

Grebes feed on small fish and other aquatic life and are strong swimmers and divers. Their toes are lobed rather than webbed. In basic (nonbreeding) plumage, Horned Grebes look like miniature, short-necked Western Grebes and spend the winter near the seashore, with a few appearing inland on large bodies of water. Nesting grounds are in Alaska, Canada, and the northern United States on freshwater ponds and marshes. This grebe's beautiful breeding plumage, rarely seen in California, features a chestnut neck and golden head plumes.

Western Grebe
Aechmophorus occidentalis 25"

The courtship antics of Western Grebes are highly animated, with pairs running rapidly upright on the water surface, side by side, then moving in circles facing one another. They breed in colonies, building floating nests anchored to reeds. They winter, often in large flocks, both along the coast and locally inland. In addition to the usual grebe diet of aquatic creatures, their own feathers are consumed in large quantities. This is the biggest of our grebes and is sometimes referred as the "swan" grebe because of its long, slender neck.

Pacific Loon, immature

Horned Grebe, winter

Western Grebe

Black-footed Albatross *Diomedea nigripes* 32", wingspread 71"

Albatrosses are the largest of seabirds, spending most of their lives over the open ocean, alighting on water only to feed on squid, fish, and carrion, or on islands to nest. They are marvelous fliers, but on land they are somewhat awkward, giving rise to their nickname "gooney birds." Black-footed Albatrosses are the most likely species to be observed in near-shore California waters and can be seen all year, but especially during summer. They often follow boats, scavenging on refuse thrown overboard. Major nesting sites are on Midway Island and other islands of the Hawaiian archipelago.

Northern Fulmar *Fulmarus glacialis* 19"

Fulmars are birds of the open ocean and members of a group of species called tube-noses, after the characteristic large nostril tubes on top of their bills. This adaptation enables these birds to drink sea water by excreting excess salt through the tubes. Fulmars range in color from dark gray to mostly white. They are abundant nesters on sea cliffs in Alaska. In northern California they occur mostly in winter, when they sometimes gather in large flocks near fishing boats. Their flight, rapid wing beats alternating with stiff-winged glides, is distinctive.

Sooty Shearwater *Puffinus griseus* 19"

The all-dark plumage combined with silvery wing linings distinguish this abundant shearwater. The term "shearwater" refers to their habit of soaring low over the water on stiff wings, using the air currents to conserve energy needed to fly. They dive and swim underwater to catch small fish, squid, and crustaceans. These birds nest during our winter on islands off southern South America, Australia, and New Zealand. They are common off the California coast through spring and summer, with fewer observed from November through March.

Black-footed Albatross

Northern Fulmar

Sooty Shearwater

Brandt's Cormorant
Phalacrocorax penicillatus 35"

Cormorants are fish-eating birds that swim low in the water and dive for their prey. White plumes on the neck and back are present only during the breeding season. Of the three common California cormorants, this is the one likely to be seen at sea in numbers. Immature birds are dark brown above and slightly paler below. This species nests in large colonies on rocky islands. A familiar sight is long lines of Brandt's Cormorants flying between feeding and roosting grounds.

Pelagic Cormorant
Phalacrocorax pelagicus 26"

This is the smallest, slimmest, and least pelagic (oceanic) of our cormorants. They nest in small colonies on rocky coastal cliffs and offshore islets. Both sexes build the nest, sharing the tasks of gathering material and arranging it; the site may be used in successive seasons. Additions added each year cause the structure to reach heights of up to six feet. White flank patches are present only during the breeding season. At other times of year, this cormorant appears dark and glossy overall, with a comparatively short, thin bill.

Brown Pelican
Pelecanus occidentalis 48"

Immatures have white bellies and plain brown necks instead of the dark bellies and distinctively marked necks of adults. It takes at least four years for young birds to reach maturity. At one time numbers of Brown Pelicans were greatly diminished because of the overuse of pesticides in agriculture. These pollutants reached the ocean in contaminated runoff water and then were absorbed by fish, becoming further concentrated within the food chain. When the pesticide-laden fish were consumed by pelicans, calcium deposition to the birds' eggshells was inhibited, resulting in extreme eggshell thinning. With reduced use of such poisons, populations of Brown Pelicans have somewhat recovered. These birds nest in colonies on islands off the coast of southern California and Mexico, moving north into northern California after the breeding season.

Brandt's Cormorant, breeding

Pelagic Cormorant, breeding

Brown Pelican, immature

Brant

Branta bernicla 25"

These geese are normally found only along the coast, where they feed almost exclusively on aquatic vegetation in shallow bays and estuaries. They have special glands that concentrate and excrete salts obtained from drinking sea water and eating saltwater plants. Brant are locally common in winter and sometimes gather in large flocks in the spring before migrating north to nesting grounds on the arctic coasts of Alaska and Canada. They usually fly low over water or along the shore in groups of around 25 individuals. They have an aversion to crossing even a narrow strip of land.

American Wigeon

Anas americana 19"

This is a common winter duck in northern California, with some remaining to nest on interior lakes at various elevations. Females are basically all brown. After the breeding season, males of this species, like many other male ducks, assume a plumage (called eclipse plumage) resembling that of females; later in fall they molt back to their breeding dress. Wigeons often graze in open grassy areas on tender shoots and grain and also feed on aquatic plants in shallow water. These ducks are sometimes called "baldpates" because of the male's white forehead and cap.

Greater Scaup

Aythya marila 18"

There are two species of ducks called scaup, Greater and Lesser, which look alike. The Greater Scaup is slightly larger and has a greenish sheen in the male's head; the heads of male Lesser Scaups have a purple sheen. However, these colors are difficult to perceive except in favorable light conditions. Female Greater and Lesser Scaups are similar, all brown with white patches at the bases of the bills. Both species are observed in northern California mostly in winter, sometimes together, but with the Greater Scaup generally preferring coastal waters. Breeding areas are in Alaska, Canada, and the northern United States. These ducks are expert divers, feeding equally on plant and animal food.

Brant

American Wigeon, male

Greater Scaup, male

Harlequin Duck
Histrionicus histrionicus 16½"

The male is one of our most beautiful ducks. Females are gray-brown with three round white spots on their heads. These uncommon ducks are most often seen in winter, usually near rugged coasts, where their main food consists of animal life (barnacles, snails, and crabs) that they dislodge from rocks. A few of these ducks nest along turbulent streams in California's high mountains, where they feed on aquatic insects. The major breeding areas are in the mountains of Alaska, Canada, and the northern United States.

White-winged Scoter
Melanitta fusca 21"

Of the three California scoters, this is the only one that shows conspicuous wing patches in all plumages when flying. The white wing patch may not always be visible on swimming birds. Females and immatures are brown with pale spots on the head. This is a fairly common duck, somewhat erratic in occurrence, seen mostly in winter; it generally prefers coastal waters. They can dive as deep as 40 feet to feed on shellfish beds, and their powerful gizzards can crush even hard-shelled oysters. Nesting grounds are in Alaska and Canada, with a few nonbreeders remaining along the California coast in summer.

Bufflehead
Bucephala albeola 13½"

This common small duck is seen in California mostly in winter, with some remaining to nest in the Cascade Mountains. Females are dark gray with small white patches on each side of their heads. Nesting habitat is northern woodlands near small lakes and ponds, where Buffleheads occupy old woodpecker holes, especially those of flickers. In the nonbreeding season, they can be seen on sheltered bays on the coast and inland rivers and lakes. These ducks are excellent divers, feeding on shrimp, other small crustaceans, and aquatic plants.

Harlequin Duck, male

White-winged Scoter, male

Bufflehead, male

Common Goldeneye
Bucephala clangula 18½"

Barrow's Goldeneye
Bucephala islandica 18"

These closely related ducks are named for their bright yellow eyes. In California, both species winter in sheltered coastal areas and inland lakes and rivers, with Barrow's being much less common and tending to stay near the ocean. There are scattered records of Common Goldeneyes in the state in summer, but for Barrow's there are only a few fall inland reports and none for summer. Differences between the species and sexes are apparent from the photograph. Their flight is swift, and their wings make a distinct whistling sound that can be heard for some distance. Wintertime food consists mostly of shellfish, sea urchins, and marine worms. Barrow's nest in wooded country in northwestern North American mountains, while the Common has a wider distribution, breeding in coniferous forests across the continent. Both species utilize natural cavities or old woodpecker holes for nesting sites.

Black-bellied Plover
Pluvialis squatarola 11½"

While in California during wintertime, this plover is gray above and white below, but as spring approaches, the striking black chest and belly of the breeding adult can be seen on some individuals before they migrate north to nesting grounds in the arctic tundra. In flight, this plover shows a white rump and dark axillaries (the innermost feathers of the underwing). Black-bellied Plovers are very common and are found on rocky shores, sandy beaches, and mudflats. They feed on marine worms, insects, and crustaceans.

Killdeer
Charadrius vociferus 10½"

This very common shorebird can be seen in a great variety of habitats, including tidal estuaries, mudflats, plowed fields, river and lake margins, grassy fields, and even lawns. Nests and eggs are well camouflaged in gravelly areas and are not easy to find even though no effort is made to conceal them. If either the nest or young is approached, one or both adults will run, feigning a broken wing to lure away the intruder. Their common alarm call, a shrill *kill-dee*, can be heard day or night. While feeding, this bird alternately runs and stands still, looking and listening, then dabs suddenly at the ground to catch an insect, its primary food.

Common and Barrow's Goldeneyes. Left to right: female Barrow's, male Common, male Barrow's, female Common.

Black-bellied Plovers

Killdeer

Black Oystercatcher

Haematopus bachmani 17½"

Oystercatchers have laterally flattened, heavy bills that are used to pry shellfish off rocks and reach into bivalve mollusks to sever muscles holding their shells closed. These birds are resident on rocky shores and islands along the coast, where they place their nests in hollows of rocks above tide line. Their coloration allows them to blend in with dark backgrounds; this, combined with slow-moving, jerky movements, makes them difficult to spot. Immatures are browner than adults and have dusky tips on their orange bills.

Willet

Catoptrophorus semipalmatus 15"

This large member of the sandpiper family is a widespread, common winter resident along the coast and sporadically in the San Joaquin Valley. Its overall drab gray appearance when standing gives no hint of the striking black-and-white pattern seen only in flight. Willets nest on the ground in open prairies of northeastern California, with a few nonbreeders remaining through the summer along the coast. Their diet includes insects, small crabs, fish, grasses, and seeds. These are conspicuous, noisy birds. When disturbed, they fly off calling a series of raucous notes over and over.

Black Oystercatcher

Willets

Willet in flight

Wandering Tattler
Heteroscelus incanus 11"

These are winter birds of rocky coasts and breakwaters. They often teeter and bob when foraging for shellfish, mollusks, and marine worms. Winter plumage is uniform gray with a pale white belly; in spring, they have blackish bars on their underparts. They nest in the mountains of Alaska above timberline. Tattlers are generally seen singly; their call is a series of clear, loud whistles, all on one pitch. In flight, these birds hold their wings stiffly, like Spotted Sandpipers.

Long-billed Curlew
Numenius americanus 23"

Long-billed Curlews are the largest North American sandpipers. Sensitive nerves in the flexible bill tip enable them to probe deeply into mud and sand to feel for and capture invertebrates such as ghost shrimp, which are swallowed whole. Winter habitats are coastal mudflats and inland agricultural fields; breeding areas are in the Great Basin prairies of northeastern California. Females average larger in size and bill length, but otherwise look like males. Large flocks of these gregarious birds can be seen and heard during migration, continuously calling *cur-lee, cur-lee.*

Marbled Godwit
Limosa fedoa 18"

Marbled Godwits are large, brown sandpipers with long, upturned bills, which they probe full length into sand and mud for worms and crustaceans. They are common winter residents along the coast and uncommon in the Central Valley. Nesting grounds are in Canadian grasslands and the northern plains region of the United States, although a few nonbreeders remain in California through the summer. These shorebirds are highly gregarious, often feeding and traveling in large flocks. Godwits were once considered gamebirds and were extirpated from many of their former haunts; with protection they have made a good, but not total, recovery.

Wandering Tattler, winter

Long-billed Curlew

Marbled Godwit

Black Turnstone
Arenaria melanocephala 9¼"

In flight, Black Turnstones show a distinctive black-and-white pattern on their backs, wings, and tails in all plumages. They frequent breakwaters, rocky beaches, and occasionally sandy shores. The name is derived from their habit of turning over beached kelp and other shore debris, which they search through for small marine organisms. This species breeds on the coastal tundra of Alaska and winters along the California coast. As is the case with many shorebirds, a few turnstones remain here during the spring and summer rather than migrate north. Breeding plumage, sometimes seen in California, is marked by white eyebrows, white spots at bases of bills, and white spotting on necks and breasts.

Surfbird
Aphriza virgata 10"

Surfbird is an apt name for this bird because during migration and in winter its habitat is wave-lashed rocks, where it feeds primarily on small mussels. Nesting takes place in rocky places above timberline in the mountains of Alaska, where the bird feeds on insects. In flight, surfbirds display a conspicuous white rump and tail, with a black band at the tip of the tail. Winter plumage is mostly gray, while breeding dress is heavily streaked and spotted with black and rufous. These birds are usually seen in small flocks, often associating with turnstones and oystercatchers.

Sanderling
Calidris alba 6½"

These pale sandpipers frequently feed along the shore on tiny marine invertebrates exposed by receding water and then are chased back by incoming waves. They prefer sandy beaches and rocky coasts and often can be approached closely. When resting, usually at high tide, up to 100 or more may gather close together above tide line. In late spring, they begin to acquire their breeding plumage of rich rufous-and-black upperparts. Sanderlings nest in the Arctic and winter on beaches all over the world.

Black Turnstone, winter

Surfbird

Sanderling

Least Sandpiper
Calidris minutilla 6"

As the name implies, this is the smallest North American sandpiper. It is one of a group of small shorebirds collectively known as "peeps." The tiny size, greenish yellow legs, and brownish plumage serve to identify this species. This common bird is observed throughout northern California during migration, and in winter it can be seen on mudflats and other wet habitats at many locations except in northeastern California and mountain areas. These sandpipers, like many others, nest on arctic tundra. They may travel singly, in pairs, or in flocks of hundreds. If the observer remains still, these birds will approach closely as they busily feed on insect larvae, crustaceans, and beach flies.

Short-billed Dowitcher
Limnodromus griseus 11"

Both Short-billed and Long-billed Dowitchers are common in California and are often found together. They closely resemble each other, and even experienced observers sometimes have difficulty separating the two. Calls are the best way to distinguish these birds. Short-bills give a mellow *tu-tu-tu*, while Long-bills make a sharp, high-pitched *keek* sound, given singly or in a rapid series. Comparing bill lengths can help, but it is not a reliable method of identification. Both species of dowitchers have white rumps and backs, long and straight bills, and similar feeding habits. Long-billed Dowitchers are common winter residents at the ocean's edge and in the Central Valley. Short-bills prefer large estuaries and are found mostly along the coast.

Red-necked Phalarope
Phalaropus lobatus 7¾"

There are three species of phalaropes that seasonally visit California, and all have similar life histories. They often spin like tops on the water surface, feeding on stirred-up larvae, crustaceans, and insects. Females are larger and more colorful in breeding plumage than males and do the courting, while males incubate the eggs and care for the chicks. Red-necked Phalaropes breed on arctic and subarctic tundra and winter chiefly at sea in the Southern Hemisphere. During migration, these phalaropes move offshore in large numbers, with tens of thousands using large inland bodies of water such as Mono Lake for staging areas, especially in fall. This species was formerly called Northern Phalarope.

Least Sandpiper

Short-billed Dowitcher, juvenile

Red-necked Phalarope, fall

Parasitic Jaeger
Stercorarius parasiticus 19"

Jaegers are agile "hawks" of the sea that frequently harass gulls and terns, forcing them to disgorge their catches, whereupon the dropped food is seized. There are three species seen regularly off the California coast, and all have complex and variable plumages ranging from pale to dark, often making identification difficult. The Parasitic Jaeger is the species most often seen from shore and even occasionally inland. They have been reported during all seasons offshore but are more common in fall. These birds nest on the arctic tundra.

Western Gull
Larus occidentalis 25"

These gulls are commonly seen year-round offshore and in the immediate vicinity of the California coast. They take about four years to reach adult plumage, with dark immatures gradually lightening to adult appearance. Western Gulls are the only gulls that nest on coastal islands and are entirely confined to land's edge, except for some individuals that wander a short distance inland to reservoirs and garbage dumps. Backs (mantles) of southern Western Gulls are black with a graduation to dark gray in northerly adults. These gulls are fond of following boats, scavenging on any refuse thrown overboard.

Glaucous-winged Gull
Larus glaucescens 26"

Glaucous-winged Gulls are similar in appearance and habits to Western Gulls. In the coastal northwestern United States, the two species hybridize extensively with each other. Some authorities consider these two gulls to be conspecific, simply representing a geographic trend from dark-mantled in the south to pale-mantled in the north. Generally, Glaucous-wings are lighter colored than Westerns in all plumages.

Parasitic Jaeger

Western Gulls

Glaucous-winged Gull, winter adult

Bonaparte's Gull   *Larus philadelphia* 13½"

An uncommon winter resident along the coast, these gulls have a buoyant, ternlike flight. Huge numbers pass the northern California shore during spring migration in April and May. They travel in tight, ball-like flocks as much as 20 miles offshore. Breeding adults have a black hood, but in winter only a black spot behind the eye is present. The summer range is from Alaska across Canada. Unlike most gulls, which are ground nesters, Bonaparte's Gulls regularly build nests in trees in spruce-fir forests. Food inland consists largely of insects or small fish, but in wintertime, near the seashore, they will eat crustaceans and marine worms and scavenge in harbors and at sewer outlets.

Heermann's Gull   *Larus heermanni* 19"

This handsome gull nests on islands off the west coast of Mexico, coming north in large numbers after the breeding season. Some remain along the coast south of San Francisco throughout the year. During their first winter, Heermann's Gulls are a deep brown, the darkest of all California's gulls. It takes three years to attain adult plumage. Their diet is varied, consisting of refuse and all kinds of marine life. They cleverly crack open shellfish by dropping them on hard surfaces. Often, several of these gulls together will harass a Brown Pelican and attempt to snatch fish from its mouth.

Ring-billed Gull   *Larus delawarensis* 17½"

This medium-sized gull has a distinctive black ring around the center of its bill. It takes only three years to attain adult plumage, instead of four for larger gulls. Winter adults have dark flecks on their heads that are lacking during the breeding season. Ring-billed Gulls are common inshore and even in urban areas, but they are rarely seen out to sea. These gulls are colonial nesters in northeastern California on islands or shores of freshwater lakes. Some non-breeding individuals remain on the California coast during summer.

Bonaparte's Gull, winter adult

Heermann's Gull, breeding

Ring-billed Gull, winter adult

Caspian Tern
Sterna caspia 21"

This bird, our largest tern, occurs on inshore coastal areas, estuaries, and freshwater lakes. In northern California, Caspian Terns nest in colonies, mainly on levees around salt evaporating ponds or in similar locations. Small fish, caught by diving into the water, make up much of their diet. The feet of terns are webbed, and though most can alight on water and float, they seldom swim because their feet are too small and weak to propel them strongly. After nesting, Caspian Terns migrate south out of northern California.

Elegant Tern
Sterna elegans 17"

Terns are closely related to gulls but appear slimmer and have a more rapid, graceful flight. Elegant Terns are postbreeding wanderers from Mexico and southern California. Large numbers of them come to northern California in late summer and fall and return south by November. This species inhabits coastal waters, harbors, and estuaries but is unreported inland and not often observed more than a few miles offshore. Winter birds have white foreheads, while breeding adults have black foreheads, crowns, and napes. The breeding plumage is rarely seen in northern California.

Common Murre
Uria aalge 17½"

Murres are members of a Northern Hemisphere family that is ecologically equivalent to the flightless southern penguins, but murres are able to fly. In California, Common Murres nest on the rocky cliffs of offshore islands and are found on both inshore waters and the open ocean. During some winter flights, when numbers are augmented by birds from northern breeding regions, they frequently occur close to shore, and occasionally inside bays and harbors. Adults in breeding plumage have an all gray-brown head. Because much of its life is spent on the ocean's surface, this species is especially vulnerable to oil spills.

Caspian Tern

Elegant Tern, winter

Common Murre, winter

Freshwater marsh, Siskiyou County

Riparian woodland, Kern County

Chapter V
Birds of Freshwater Wetlands and Riparian Woodlands

Fresh water is of extreme importance to most birds. Freshwater wetlands and riparian (streamside) woodlands are widely distributed and commonly adjacent to arid locales. Species not normally considered wetland inhabitants are often attracted to these habitats by available food, cover, and especially water. Marshes may be found wherever fresh water is standing or flowing slowly enough so that aquatic plants can take root. Marshes can also occur along edges of streams and rivers. These areas are more important for nesting purposes than open water. Most of the birds nesting in this habitat are so specialized that they can live nowhere else. Riparian woodlands include trees and shrubs that border streams, rivers, and small bodies of water. This habitat is widely scattered, and therefore species favoring these areas have noncontiguous ranges.

As with coastal salt marshes, many wetlands have been polluted or destroyed by unrestricted development, landfills, drainage, and urban use. Fortunately, this destruction has been somewhat mitigated by creation of artificial lakes, reservoirs, ponds, and even sewage facilities, although most riparian woodland habitat is so highly specialized that nothing can really make up for the continuing loss of this ecosystem.

Throughout California, the best places to see great masses of birds are in wetlands. The sights and sounds of huge flocks of waterfowl and swarms of shorebirds, in season, wheeling and turning in coordinated flight, are truly awesome and inspiring. Perhaps the optimum time to observe birds here, especially shy species like rails, is early morning just after dawn, when many individuals are in plain view, conspicuously feeding, displaying, or calling.

Many species discussed in Chapter IV, Birds of the Coast and Nearby Ocean, can regularly be found in similar environments away from the shore, especially in migration.

Common Loon
Gavia immer 32"

In fall and winter, Common Loons appear to be plain, dark gray birds with pale underparts, but in late spring they attain their elegant breeding plumage, as pictured. A few have been known to nest on large lakes in northern California, but the major breeding areas are in Alaska, across Canada, and along the northern edge of the United States. Of the three species of loons that regularly winter along the California coast, Common Loons are the largest and the species most likely to be seen inland. The expression "crazy as a loon" is based on the loud, undulating, laughterlike yodel given during the nesting season.

Pied-billed Grebe
Podilymbus podiceps 13½"

Pied-billed Grebes are small, brown, ducklike birds commonly seen on freshwater ponds and lakes. "Pied" refers to the dark and light markings on the bills of breeding adults. Winter birds lose the bill markings and black chin. When feeding underwater or when disturbed, grebes are capable of diving and swimming 100 feet or more beneath the surface, staying submerged as long as one minute. Other times, they may slowly sink, leaving scarcely a ripple on the surface. They build concealed, floating nests in which up to 10 dull white eggs are laid. In winter these birds also frequent saltwater bays and inlets along the coast.

American White Pelican
Pelecanus erythrorhynchos 62"

Unlike their brown relatives, White Pelicans prefer inland waters to those along the coast, but they are observed occasionally on coastal bays and lagoons in winter. They often fly on their 10-foot wingspreads in formation like geese or soar on thermals to great altitudes like vultures. White Pelicans are colonial nesters on islands in freshwater lakes of the western United States and Canada. These largest of North American birds frequently feed by swimming in closely coordinated formations, scooping up fish they have driven into shallow water.

Common Loon, breeding

Pied-billed Grebe, breeding

American White Pelican

Double-crested Cormorant   *Phalacrocorax auritus* 32"

Of the three common California cormorants observed along the coast, this is the only one that is also found on interior bodies of water. Head plumes are present only in breeding season and are usually white on coastal birds and black on inland ones. Immature birds are brown with pale underparts. Relatives of this species are the guano birds of South America, while in some Asian countries captive cormorants have been used to catch fish. Cormorant feathers are not completely waterproof, so the birds have to frequently dry out by facing the sun and spreading their wings. Double-crested Cormorants fly with distinctive crooks in their necks, while other cormorants fly with outstretched necks.

American Bittern   *Botaurus lentiginosus* 28"

This member of the heron family is not a frequent nester in northern California but is fairly common in the winter, when local birds are joined by migrants from farther north. Its cryptic plumage coloration and pattern make it difficult to observe in dense marsh vegetation. When flushed, it flies off with wings flopping loosely and feet dangling, often uttering a harsh croak as it picks up speed. If discovered when standing in the open, or if it senses it is being watched, this bird assumes a position with its bill pointed up and body contracted, appearing to be a stake in the reeds.

Great Blue Heron   *Ardea herodias* 46"

Great Blue Herons are often mistakenly called cranes. Herons fly with deep, graceful wing beats and their necks folded, whereas cranes have shallow wing beats and hold their necks straight out. Nests are flimsy platforms of sticks and grass built in trees or occasionally on the ground. They are refurbished each season and used year after year. These birds hunt, day or night, by standing motionless waiting for fish, frogs, insects, snakes, and even gophers to come within striking distance. At other times, they stealthily stalk their prey.

Double-crested Cormorant

American Bittern

Great Blue Heron

Great Egret
Casmerodius albus 39"

The name "egret" is applied to most white species of herons. Great Egrets can be identified by their yellow bill and large size and are found worldwide. Flowing white back plumes are present only in the breeding season. This egret tends to be more solitary than the smaller, similar Snowy Egret, but does nest in loose colonies along with other egrets and herons. Great Egrets frequent both salt- and freshwater marshes, where they feed by stalking in shallow water or on land for fish, insects, snakes, and even rodents.

Snowy Egret
Egretta thula 24"

The black bill and distinctive bright yellow toes with contrasting black legs make this small member of the heron family easy to identify. Long head and back plumes are present only in breeding plumage. Snowy Egrets nest in colonies, along with other species of wading birds, in trees or brush on islands or over water. After the nesting season they disperse widely to lower-elevation wetlands and the seashore. Small aquatic life, such as frogs, fish, and insects, forms a major part of this egret's diet.

Green Heron
Butorides virescens 18"

These solitary birds can be seen stealthily stalking their aquatic prey in quiet waters. If alarmed, this small heron stretches its neck, elevates its crest, and nervously jerks its tail. When flushed, it often flies off emitting an explosive *sky-owk*. Green Herons prefer to hunt and nest in dense riparian growth rather than more open areas. Young birds are browner above than adults and have heavily streaked underparts. These herons have a wide distribution most of the year, with some withdrawal in winter to central and southern parts of California. This species is sometimes called Green-backed Heron.

Great Egret

Snowy Egret

Green Heron

Black-crowned Night-Heron   *Nycticorax nycticorax* 25"

This heron is largely, but not strictly, nocturnal and is common near freshwater ponds, swamps, and tidal marshes throughout the world. Sometimes these birds fly out over water, alight on the surface, and swim in their search for food. They nest in colonies in trees, cattails, and clumps of tall grass, where groups composed of young birds and adults are often seen roosting together during daytime. Night-herons are extremely opportunistic and thrive by occupying marginal habitats and eating a wider variety of food than other herons. Immatures are mostly brown with streaks and spots of white and buff.

White-faced Ibis   *Plegadis chihi* 23"

The white border around bare facial skin, from which this species derives its name, is present only in breeding season. Numbers of these birds have declined over the years, with only small, scattered nesting colonies remaining in northern California. During winter, they can regularly be found only near Los Banos in the San Joaquin Valley. White-faced Ibises require extensive marshes for breeding and large flooded fields for feeding. Ibises fly in diagonal lines or V formations, alternately flapping and soaring.

Tundra Swan   *Cygnus columbianus* 52"

Formerly called Whistling Swan, the Tundra Swan occurs throughout the Northern Hemisphere, with breeding grounds on the arctic tundra. In California, some winter along the coast but most spend the season on refuges and agricultural lands in the Central Valley. Tundra Swans mate for life and usually nest in the same place year after year. Young birds are gray-brown with pinkish bills. Swans feed on aquatic vegetation by tipping up and reaching underwater with their long necks. When migrating, usually at night, flocks of these birds fly in V-shaped wedges at great altitudes, sometimes as high as 7,000 feet.

132

Black-crowned Night-Heron, adult

White-faced Ibis, winter

Tundra Swans

Greater White-fronted Goose   *Anser albifrons* 28"

This goose is named for the white band at the base of the bill of the adult. It is also sometimes called "speckle belly" because of the heavy barring on its underparts. Young birds lack the white front and black lower markings. Breeding grounds are on the arctic tundra of Alaska and Canada, with large numbers spending the winter in the Central Valley. This goose is primarily a grazer, feeding on marsh grass and fresh growth in burned-over pastures along with waste grain and aquatic plants.

Snow Goose   *Chen caerulescens* 28"

The white form of this bird is by far the most common one seen in California. At one time the dark morph was considered a separate species, called Blue Goose, until research proved the two types are conspecific. Snow Geese winter in huge flocks in the Central Valley on various federal and state waterfowl refuges, with smaller numbers scattered throughout the state and along the coast. Like most geese, Snow Geese breed on the arctic tundra. During winter, they feed in large fields and roost on open bodies of water, consuming large quantities of seed and grain along with aquatic plants of all kinds.

Cinnamon Teal   *Anas cyanoptera* 16"

Female and male Cinnamon Teals in eclipse (postbreeding) plumage look much like females of other small duck species. This species is a common migrant and summer resident in freshwater marshes and coastal estuaries. Cinnamon Teal have conspicuous large blue patches on their forewings, easily seen in flight. Their nests are built on the ground, concealed in tall grass or weeds and lined with down. They will also place nests in thick reeds just above water. Although a dabbling duck, they seldom tip up as other ducks do, instead preferring to skim the water with their bills or reach for plant food below the surface.

Greater White-fronted Goose

Snow Geese, white (left) and blue morphs

Cinnamon Teal, male

Canvasback
Aythya valisineria 21"

Canvasbacks superficially resemble Redheads but can be distinguished by their sloping foreheads and long black bills. Females have pale brown heads and necks with dusky backs and sides. They are common winter visitors to California, with a few nesting in scattered localities in the interior. These ducks are declining in number because their primary breeding habitat, potholes of North American prairies, is diminishing due to draining and development for agriculture. Canvasbacks are divers and feed on the bottom of shallow lakes and ponds, straining seeds from mud or pulling up roots of aquatic plants. These ducks migrate at high altitudes and great speed in large V-shaped flocks.

Redhead
Aythya americana 19"

Redheads are similar in appearance to Canvasbacks but have rounded heads and tricolored bills. Males have gray, not whitish, backs. Redheads are locally common, but they are not as abundant as Canvasbacks. A few nest in California, but the main breeding grounds are in other western states and Canada on large lakes with emergent marshes. Redheads are active birds, feeding in morning, evening, and often at night. They dive as far as 10 feet below the surface for aquatic plants in fresh water and for shellfish in brackish water. These ducks have been known to crossbreed in the wild with other species, such as Ring-necked Ducks and the two scaups.

Common Merganser
Mergus merganser 25"

Mergansers are diving ducks whose long thin bills have toothlike serrations that enable them to catch and hold fish, crustaceans, and aquatic insects. Females have a chestnut crested head and white chin. Common Mergansers nest in holes and cavities of trees in woodlands near lakes and rivers, but in winter they also may be found on brackish water. In taking flight, mergansers run along the water's surface, beating their wings for a considerable distance before becoming airborne. These are the largest North American ducks that are found inland.

Canvasback, male

Redhead

Common Merganser, male

Osprey
Pandion haliaetus 23½", wingspread 65"

Ospreys are often called "fish hawks" because of their ability to catch fish. They hunt by hovering with slow wing flaps and then quickly plunging into the water, seizing their prey with strong talons. Nests are usually built high in dead snags but occasionally are placed on the ground. The same locations are used from year to year, with fresh branches added each season. In northern California, Ospreys are regularly observed in summer along the shore and in the Coast Ranges north of San Francisco Bay. A few pairs nest east of the Sierra Nevada in places like Mono Lake. During migration, they can also be seen in other parts of the state.

Bald Eagle
Haliaeetus leucocephalus 34", wingspread 80"

It takes four to five years for Bald Eagles to attain their white heads and tails. Young birds are dark brown with pale splotches. Our national symbol can be seen at scattered locations in California along rivers and large lakes, mainly in winter. They are most common in the extreme northern part of the state, with scattered nesting sites in mountainous areas. They feed largely on fish, seizing them at the water's surface or taking them from Ospreys. Eagles also prey on waterfowl and coots and will eat carrion. Fully protected by law, these magnificent birds are barely maintaining their small population in spite of habitat destruction and human harassment.

Sora
Porzana carolina 8¾"

Although not often seen, Soras are common and can be frequently heard uttering a rapid, descending whinny that levels off at the end. Sometimes this rail can be watched at the edges of grain fields or freshwater and brackish marshes, daintily stepping over mud, out in the open, picking up small mollusks and aquatic insects. But if alarmed it runs for cover, quickly slipping out of sight into the dense vegetation. Soras readily swim and easily run through shallow water.

Osprey

Bald Eagle

Sora

Black-necked Stilt
Himantopus mexicanus 14"

Stilts are conspicuous shorebirds of estuaries, lakeshores, mud-flats, and salt ponds and can be seen throughout the year busily searching for insects and crustaceans in shallow water. Females and young have brownish backs instead of the black on males. Nests are slight, unconcealed depressions on the ground, and young are able to feed and take care of themselves soon after hatching. If an intruder approaches a mixed flock of these birds and other shore-birds, stilts are usually the first to fly, loudly and persistently sounding the alarm.

American Avocet
Recurvirostra americana 18"

The rust color on the head and neck of breeding adults is replaced by grayish white in winter. The most obvious sexual difference is that the male's bill is longer and straighter than the female's. Avocets often feed in small flocks in shallow water, sweeping their bills from side to side, stirring up aquatic insects. In deeper water, they dabble and swim like ducks. Gathering in groups, pairs perform elaborate courtship displays, and later, eggs are laid in slight hollows lined with a few dry grasses on sun-baked flats and marshes bordering shallow lakes.

Greater Yellowlegs
Tringa melanoleuca 14"

There are two species of yellowlegs seen in California, with the Greater being larger and much more common than the Lesser Yellowlegs. Both are rare in June, but southbound migrants appear by July. White tails on both birds are conspicuous in flight. This large sandpiper nests in wetlands and muskegs across the taiga zone of Alaska and Canada and winters on coastal mudflats, marshes, and inland lakeshores singly or in small noisy flocks. A common call is a loud, descending series of three or more *tew* notes. In spite of their long bills, Greater Yellowlegs do not probe but instead peck or dab and swing their bills to catch aquatic life.

Black-necked Stilt, male

American Avocets

Greater Yellowlegs

Spotted Sandpiper
Actitis macularia 7½"

In breeding plumage, Spotted Sandpipers are heavily spotted below, but during winter they are not spotted (as pictured). They are usually solitary, and when approached fly off with stiff, rapid wing beats interspersed with short glides. While feeding, this sandpiper continually bobs and teeters as it walks along sheltered streams, ponds, lakes, and marshes. Nests are placed in saucer-shaped hollows on the ground and often hidden in grass, with locations ranging from lowland riverbeds to high mountain ponds. Females are the more aggressive sex—they hold territories, display to males, and often have more than one mate.

Common Snipe
Gallinago gallinago 10½"

Snipe are locally common but not often seen, staying well hidden along marshy edges of streams and ponds and in wet meadows. When disturbed, they take off suddenly in a rapid zigzag flight and drop quickly out of sight some distance away. Breeding grounds in California are in the mountains and Great Basin region; in winter snipe move to lower elevations, westward as far as the coast. They feed by plunging their highly sensitive bills straight down into mud to probe for earthworms, insect larvae, and other aquatic life.

Forster's Tern
Sterna forsteri 14½"

This tern has a black cap only in breeding plumage. It nests in colonies on sandy areas with scattered bushes at the coast and in marshes and on floating debris of interior lakes. These terns dive for small fish but also sweep gracefully through the air to catch flying insects or swoop over the surface of the water to pick up floating dead bugs. This is California's most common summer tern, although there are several similar species, identifiable with practice, present during migration. Forster's Terns are the only terns normally found in northern California during winter.

142

Spotted Sandpiper, winter

Common Snipe

Forster's Tern, winter

Black Tern
Chlidonias niger 9¾"

Black Terns mostly breed north of California, with only a few scattered colonies in marshes of the upper part of the state's interior. Two years are required to attain the adult's black breeding plumage; winter and young birds appear almost all grayish white or patchy black and white. Nests are shallow cups on floating dead plants or in loosely assembled reeds just above water. On their breeding grounds, these terns feed mainly on insects, but as they migrate to South America for the winter their food consists of fish and other marine life.

Belted Kingfisher
Ceryle alcyon 13"

Males have only a blue-gray breast band and lack the additional rusty band and rufous flanks of females. Kingfishers are typical wetland birds and can be seen in all seasons but are extremely wary. Their large size and big, ragged crests make these birds easy to identify. They nest in burrows, dug several feet into dirt banks near water. Fish, frogs, crayfish, and aquatic insects are caught by headlong dives into water that may be only a few inches deep. Their call is a loud, harsh rattle, frequently given in flight.

Black Phoebe
Sayornis nigricans 6¾"

Black Phoebes are members of the flycatcher family and frequent brushy or wooded areas near fresh water. They typically catch insects by sallying forth from a favorite perch. Nests are made of mud and are often built on building ledges or under bridges. When perched, phoebes flick their tails up, down, and sideways. This species does not migrate, but there is some limited movement after nesting. Young birds have brown feathers mixed with the predominant black ones. A common call is *tsip,* or a more prolonged and plaintive *tsee-ee.*

Black Tern, breeding

Belted Kingfisher, female

Black Phoebe

Cistothorus palustris 5"

common residents of both salt- and freshwater
often hard to see because they stay hidden in
out in breeding season males will climb a tall reed
loud trills, gurgles, and rattles, repeated over and
arge, ball-shaped affairs with side entrances, built
above water or the ground by females. Males often
construe o six dummy nests. Some males have more than one
mate, with each female occupying a small part of the larger territory
controlled by her consort.

Yellow Warbler
Dendroica petechia 5"

Except in migration, Yellow Warblers are strictly residents of
riparian woodlands. Nests are built in a fork of a tree or shrub from
just above the ground to almost treetop level. Yellow Warblers are
frequently parasitized by cowbirds, but many times, after a cowbird
egg is deposited in its nest, the warbler will build a second nest on
top of the first and lay a second clutch. However, if there is a Red-
winged Blackbird colony nearby, the blackbirds will often drive off
cowbirds. The male's distinct reddish streaks on the underparts are
faint or absent in females.

Common Yellowthroat
Geothlypis trichas 5"

This member of the wood warbler family breeds in interior freshwater and coastal saltwater marshes and moist, weedy fields, with
males often mating with more than one female. During migration,
yellowthroats can be found in a wide variety of habitats, including
dense riparian growth, lake margins, and brush. Females lack the
males' black mask. Although these birds are usually difficult to see
in thick vegetation, males frequently climb to an exposed perch and
sing continuously, *twitchity-twitchity-twitchity.*

Marsh Wren

Yellow Warbler, male

Common Yellowthroat, male

Song Sparrow

Melospiza melodia 6¼"

There are a number of subspecies (races) of Song Sparrows, both breeding residents and winter visitors to California. All have the same basic plumage pattern, with varying shades of grays and browns, and usually can not be differentiated in the field. However, some of these races are highly specialized and require particular habitats. For example, the Song Sparrow forms that nest in the marshes of San Francisco Bay are considered endangered because of the intensive development of that region. Other Song Sparrows are more common and can be found in dense riparian thickets and marshes throughout the state. The typical song is a loud, bright series of three or four long notes followed by short notes and trills.

Red-winged Blackbird

Agelaius phoeniceus 8¾"

This blackbird is a conspicuous resident of freshwater marshes, wet fields, and roadside sloughs throughout California. Females and young are brown with distinct black stripes on the underparts, and immature males are brown with an often-concealed orange shoulder patch. These birds are colonial nesters and, after breeding, gather in large flocks along with other species of blackbirds. Red-winged Blackbirds are extremely vocal, often emitting harsh *chak* calls and a liquid series of notes ending in a trill sounding like *con-ker-lee*.

Yellow-headed Blackbird

Xanthocephalus xanthocephalus 9½"

The habits of the Yellow-headed Blackbird are similar to those of the closely related Red-winged Blackbird, but Yellow-headeds are not as abundant. Males will drive off and exclude Red-winged Blackbirds from the Yellow-headeds' area of the marsh, which is usually cattails or bulrushes over standing water. Females have yellow only on their throats and chests and lack the males' white wing patches. After nesting, these blackbirds gather in flocks, but virtually all leave northern California in winter.

Song Sparrow

Red-winged Blackbird, male

Yellow-headed Blackbird, male

Great Basin sagebrush habitat, Modoc County

Pinyon-juniper woodland, Inyo County

Chapter VI
Birds East of the Sierra Nevada

This chapter includes those regions of northern California eastward from the Cascade Range and Sierra Nevada to the Nevada border. Major topographic features are the Modoc Plateau, Great Basin, Mono Lake, and Death Valley, along with several high mountain ranges such as the Warner and White Mountains. Birdlife of higher elevations is discussed in Chapter III.

Much of this eastern section of the state is characterized by desert valleys and arid ranges running generally north and south. Part of the area is considered an extension of the Great Basin, a vast semiarid region stretching to the Rocky Mountains. Desertlike conditions prevail because moisture coming from the Pacific Ocean is blocked by the Cascades and Sierra Nevada. Annual precipitation, occurring mostly in winter but with some summer showers, varies from 5 to 20 inches depending on location. Ancient volcanic activity is evident in many localities, and summers are hot and dry, exacerbated by strong winds resulting in a high rate of evaporation.

Great Basin elevations range from about 2,000 feet to over 13,000 feet. Higher altitudes have the usual boreal forests and other mountainous habitats. Foothills and ridges are covered with dwarf coniferous forests of pinyon pine and juniper. Lower elevations contain tablelands covered with sagebrush and other typical high-desert vegetation. Interspersed with these biotic communities are grasslands, seasonal marshes, shallow ponds, and a few rivers bordered by riparian habitat. Usually dry lake beds, encrusted with mineral salts, sometimes contain water for a short time, but it quickly evaporates because of the very dry climate. On the rare occasions these alkali lakes do have water, they attract large numbers of migrating birds.

Although this region contains many marvelous vistas of spectacular scenery, coloration of flora is mostly muted shades of green, gray, and brown, resulting in resident birds evolving plumage of similar hues, making observation of birdlife somewhat difficult. However, in spite of harsh climatic conditions, this sparsely populated region of California does embrace a rich, diverse variety of birdlife, including several specialized species such as the Sage Grouse, Gray Flycatcher, Pinyon Jay, and Sage Thrasher.

Many authorities consider Death Valley and vicinity as part of southern California because its avifauna is similar to that of southern California's low deserts. However, it is included here because it lies north of the line I have arbitrarily used to separate the state into two portions, northern and southern.

Mono Lake, Mono County

Green-winged Teal
Anas crecca 14½"

This small duck is common in winter along the coast and in the Central Valley. It nests regularly in the Great Basin region of California. The bright green wing patches, most visible in flight, are good field marks in all plumages. Two other species of teal (Cinnamon and Blue-winged) frequent California, but both have blue forewing patches. The females of all three species are brown overall and difficult to identify, especially when standing or swimming. However, breeding teal males are easily told, each having distinct body plumage. This species' typical diet of aquatic plants and animals is augmented in fall by berries and nuts gathered from woods and meadows. Green-winged Teal can walk easily on land and often travel long distances in search of food. Nests are sometimes a quarter of a mile from water. They are depressions on the ground in clumps of grass and are lined with weeds, feathers, and down.

Golden Eagle
Aquila chrysaetos 35", wingspread 84"

Despite its great size, the Golden Eagle is one of the most graceful birds of prey, soaring for hours with little apparent effort. When sighting a target, often a large rodent or rabbit, it can dive at a speed said to reach up to 100 miles an hour. These eagles have been known to capture flying birds as big as geese and cranes. In California, these birds are most common east of the Sierra Nevada, but they are occasionally seen in the high and coastal mountains and in the Central Valley. Only adults have the golden hue on their head and neck feathers from which this species gets its name. Young birds have white patches in their wings and white in the tail.

Green-winged Teal, male

Green-winged Teal, female

Golden Eagle

Ferruginous Hawk

Buteo regalis 23", wingspread 53"

Many large hawks have two color forms (morphs), light or dark, with the dark (called melanistic) being the least common and most difficult to identify. This species is an uncommon but regular winter visitor throughout much of California, especially east of the Sierra Nevada and in the grassy hills of the Coast Ranges. It is often seen sitting quietly in a low tree, on a fence post, or even on the ground watching for prey, which consists of ground squirrels, rabbits, and insects. "Ferruginous" refers to the dark reddish color on the legs of adult birds, which in flight can be seen as a V shape against their pale underparts.

Chukar

Alectoris chukar 14"

This is an introduced gamebird whose natural range is arid, rocky deserts of India and Turkey. It is now successfully established in eastern California in sagebrush grasslands and on rocky, brushy slopes of dry mountains and rugged canyons. These birds are usually wary and will run instead of fly if they perceive danger. Chukars forage widely for seeds, fruit, and leaves of weeds, mainly during midmorning and into the afternoon, later making daily trips to watering places. This bird is a rare instance of an introduced exotic species that has apparently not had a detrimental effect on native flora or fauna.

Ferruginous Hawk, light morph

Ferruginous Hawk, dark morph

Chukar

Sage Grouse
Centrocercus urophasianus 28"

The courtship display of the male Sage Grouse is one of the most fascinating performances of the bird world. Just before dawn, in early spring, groups of males gather in a favored open area on a sagebrush plain, each vying for a desirable spot. There they puff out air sacs located on their necks, extend their breast feathers, and erect and spread their tail feathers. Wings are drooped forward and shaken vigorously as the bird struts and prances, intermittently emitting popping noises as air is released from the sacs. After a time, the smaller, plainer females emerge from the surrounding vegetation to mate and feed among the strutting males. Regrettably, numbers of this magnificent grouse have been declining because its specialized habitat has been subjected to heavy livestock grazing and agricultural development.

Wilson's Phalarope
Phalaropus tricolor 9¼"

Wilson's Phalaropes are seen regularly in interior portions of California and are the only phalaropes that do not breed on the arctic tundra. Although nesting and food requirements are much the same as for other phalaropes, this species tends to feed more on land than its relatives. In fall, these birds are mostly gray and white, displaying a distinctive white rump and tail in flight. Nests are grass-lined depressions on the ground in moist or arid Great Basin and prairie country. En route to and from their wintering grounds in South America, thousands of these birds gather on Mono Lake to rest and feed on abundant brine flies.

California Gull
Larus californicus 21"

California Gulls are the gulls responsible for saving the crops of Utah's early Mormon settlers by devouring hordes of invading insects. These birds nest on lakes and marshes throughout the Great Basin, with California's major colony located at Mono Lake. In winter, they move to fields and lakes throughout the rest of California. They are especially common along the coast and out to sea and are frequently seen flying over urban areas. Young birds are dark brown and are difficult to distinguish from immatures of other gull species.

Sage Grouse, male

Wilson's Phalaropes, male and female

California Gull, breeding adult

Greater Roadrunner   *Geococcyx californianus* 23"

Although considered to be birds of the southern California desert, roadrunners can also be found in scattered brushy localities along the coast to Del Norte County and north to Shasta County in the interior. They are absent on the floor of the Central Valley and rare east of the Sierra Nevada. This bird is a member of the cuckoo family and, although able to fly, prefers to run on the ground. Diet is varied and includes insects, scorpions, lizards, snakes, and mice. The call is dovelike, consisting of low, mellow notes running down the scale, and can be heard at great distances.

Long-eared Owl   *Asio otus* 15"

Although primarily nocturnal, Long-eared Owls can sometimes be found in the daytime roosting in dense groves of trees, where they raise their ear tufts high and compress their feathers close to their body to resemble an upright stub. They nest in old hawk, raven, and crow nests or in cavities of old stumps. Winter roosts can contain up to two dozen individuals. These owls are skillful hunters, flying over open ground from dusk to dawn, especially on moonlit nights, feeding on rodents of all kinds and occasionally birds.

Common Poorwill   *Phalaenoptilus nuttallii* 7¾"

Poorwills are strictly nocturnal and are closely related to nighthawks. They feed on flying insects by sallying up from the ground and returning to nearly the same spot with their prey. These birds live in open areas of mixed chaparral-grassland and sagebrush. The nest is a bare scrape in the ground, sometimes partly shaded by a bush or tuft of grass. Most poorwills winter from central California south to Mexico, but some individuals do not migrate and are known to hibernate (a rare trait in birds) through the coldest season. Females closely resemble males but have tail feathers more narrowly tipped with white. The name "poorwill" alludes to its melancholy cry, which can be heard at dusk and through the night from some distance.

Greater Roadrunner

Long-eared Owl

Common Poorwill, male

Gray Flycatcher
Empidonax wrightii 6"

The breeding habitat of the Gray Flycatcher is tall sagebrush, pinyon-juniper woodland, and open arid forest, but during migration it can be found in small numbers throughout California at lower elevations. This species is generally the palest and least yellow of our small flycatchers. When perched, it drops its tail slowly downward like a phoebe, rather than jerking it up spasmodically like most of its relatives. Its winter range is from southern California through northwestern Mexico.

Say's Phoebe
Sayornis saya 7½"

Say's Phoebes are flycatchers and catch their food in typical flycatcher fashion. These birds are fairly common in dry open country and sagebrush plains, generally avoiding timbered places. They frequently pump and spread their tails when perched. Nests are built on ledges in buildings or in crevices of cliffs. Most individuals spend winter in California, with numbers augmented by birds from the north. Their most common call is a soft, mournful, descending *chu-weer.*

Pinyon Jay
Gymnorhinus cyanocephalus 10½"

Pinyon Jays resemble small, all-blue crows. After the nesting season, they gather in noisy flocks numbering into hundreds of individuals. They have complex social organizations, with tightly knit integrated groups often traveling together. Their movements are dictated by weather and food supply. They are mainly confined to eastern California, and are found sporadically in pinyon-juniper woodlands where they feed on pinyon-pine nuts, grain, insects, and berries. A typical flight call is a laughing *hah-hah* sound, audible over long distances.

Gray Flycatcher

Say's Phoebe

Pinyon Jay

Black-billed Magpie

Pica pica 19"

Magpies are close relatives of crows and jays and occur throughout most of the Northern Hemisphere. In California, this species can be found only in the northern and eastern edges of the state. This conspicuous bird can be readily identified by its black-and-white plumage and unusually long, iridescent tail. Nests are built in small, scattered colonies in thickets, frequently along streams. Males bring in nest materials and females build the nest. Habits are much the same as those of the Yellow-billed Magpie, described in Chapter II.

Common Raven

Corvus corax 24"

Often confused with crows, ravens are larger and have shaggy neck feathers and wedge-shaped tails instead of the rounded tails of crows. Ravens are aggressive, resourceful birds whose range and numbers are increasing in many parts of California. They soar, sometimes in large numbers, like hawks and vultures, riding thermals high in the sky. Habitats of this bird are varied, ranging from high in the mountains down to the coast and from arid regions to those with heavy rainfall. Ravens scavenge roadkills and eat a wide variety of plant and animal food. They utter many different sounds, including croaks, gurgling notes, and bell-like tones.

Sage Thrasher

Oreoscoptes montanus 8½"

Sage Thrashers are typical breeding birds of the dry sagebrush plains of eastern California. Males, in early spring, sing a soft mockingbird-like song from the tops of tall perches. In fall, most individuals migrate southward to northern Mexico, although there are scattered winter records of this bird from central and southern parts of the state. These thrashers are usually shy and difficult to approach. They frequently run over the ground like robins, but unlike robins they habitually stay in dense brush, foraging for insects, spiders, and berries.

Black-billed Magpie

Common Raven

Sage Thrasher

Black-throated Gray Warbler   *Dendroica nigrescens* 5"

Black-throated Gray Warblers are locally common breeding residents at lower elevations in arid eastern California forests and in wooded mountain ranges elsewhere in the state; they are widespread in other habitats during migration. Females and immatures have less extensive black bibs than adult males. These warblers forage among leaves and bushes for insects and are especially fond of oakworms and other green caterpillars. They are seen singly or in mixed feeding groups of other small birds. The song is a lazy, drawling *wee-zy, wee-zy, wee-zy-weet*.

Brewer's Sparrow   *Spizella breweri* 5½"

This typical bird of arid sagebrush flats is a shy, retiring species, often difficult to see except when the male perches on a tall bush and sings a series of buzzy, sustained, canary-like trills, one of the most conspicuous sounds of sagebrush country. Many males sing in chorus at dawn and at twilight on nesting grounds. During spring and summer, these sparrows feed mostly on insects, but in fall and winter they consume weed seeds, deriving needed moisture from their food. Their winter range is from southern California east to Texas and south to Mexico.

Sage Sparrow   *Amphispiza belli* 6¼"

The Sage Sparrow is another grayish bird found in eastern California sagebrush communities, although it also occurs in similar shrubby habitats of the Coast Ranges. Typically, this sparrow is difficult to see because of its habits of running on the ground, tail cocked, and flying low between bushes. Often the male will sing a series of weak, high-pitched tinkling notes from the top of a bush while twitching and waving its dark tail. Cuplike nests are well hidden, built close to the ground in thick brush.

Black-throated Gray Warbler, male

Brewer's Sparrow

Sage Sparrow

Listed below are some additional birds, described in other chapters, that can often be found in specialized habitats in eastern California. Species and numbers greatly increase during migration.

Species	Preferred Locality
American White Pelican	large lakes
Turkey Vulture	open country
Red-tailed Hawk	open country
Mourning Dove	open country
Great Horned Owl	open woodlands and canyons
Western Kingbird	scattered trees, fences
Violet-green Swallow	pinyon-juniper woodlands
Plain Titmouse	pinyon-juniper woodlands
Bushtit	pinyon-juniper woodlands
White-breasted Nuthatch	woodlands
House Wren	open woodlands
Bewick's Wren	open woodlands and scrub
Mountain Bluebird	scattered trees and fields
Loggerhead Shrike	scattered large bushes
Yellow-rumped Warbler	forests and open woodlands
Northern Oriole	open deciduous woodlands
Western Meadowlark	open countryside
various waterbirds and shorebirds	lakes and marshes
Green-tailed Towhee	sagebrush in pinyon-juniper woodlands

Tidal salt marsh remnant at San Francisco Bay, San Mateo County. Vegetation is mostly cordgrass.

Tidal flats at Morro Bay, San Luis Obispo County. Vegetation here is mainly pickleweed.

Total and permanent destruction of a redwood forest in Del Norte County by clear-cutting.

Chapter VII
Endangered Birds

Several bird species once observed frequently or at least regularly in northern California are now becoming scarce or may be absent altogether. Only a few remnant populations of some of these endangered birds can still be found in suitable habitats. The primary cause of this situation is rapid destruction of the birds' breeding grounds. Some birds are so specialized that they cannot adapt to new conditions or move elsewhere. If precise habitat requisites are not preserved, certain species will be extirpated forever.

Among the dangers constantly faced by these special creatures are the threat of disasters such as oil spills, poorly restricted development, and pollution. Some birds are so scarce that entire populations could be wiped out quickly by any one of these forces. In addition, native predators such as raccoons, coyotes, and cowbirds, whose populations have exploded because of human disturbance of the environment, constantly harass shy and helpless birds.

Perhaps the greatest predator danger is from introduced red foxes, which are especially fond of eating ground-nesting birds. Also, many people do not realize the damage that freely roaming house cats inflict on birds. Severe measures must be taken to control these non-native predators if we are to preserve native bird species now barely surviving. A hopeful sign is that increasing numbers of people are becoming aware that we must preserve the natural environment not only to protect distinctive plant and animal life, but to maintain our quality of life as well.

Peregrine Falcon
Falco peregrinus 18"

These magnificent falcons have suffered greatly from habitat destruction, harmful pesticides, and collecting by falconers. There is a fairly successful program of reintroducing birds bred and raised in captivity into the wild, but even released individuals are in constant danger of harm from ever-present human dangers as well as natural ones. Peregrines inhabit open country, often near cliffs, wherever there is an abundance of waterfowl, shorebirds, or colonial seabirds; they may even nest among high office buildings in cities, where they feed on pigeons. They are one of the fastest-flying birds, attaining speeds up to 60 miles per hour in level flight and 175 miles per hour in dives. As with many birds of prey, females are considerably larger than males.

Clapper Rail
Rallus longirostris 14½"

There are a number of subspecies of Clapper Rails that occur in North America, but only one is found in northern California. The California race breeds in the extensive saltwater marshes that margin San Francisco Bay, where its habitat is in danger from pollution and unrestricted development and introduced red foxes threaten its welfare. This rail is now extirpated from other coastal areas where it was formerly common. The Clapper Rail's usual call, heard chiefly at dusk and dawn, is a series of dry *kek* notes, accelerating and then slowing, but any sudden loud sound may startle several of these birds at any time into a chorus of chattering calls. Clapper Rails swim well and can run rapidly through dense marsh vegetation with the greatest of ease. Often they are quite tame, and if watched quietly, especially at low tide, they will walk about and feed in the open for considerable lengths of time.

Peregrine Falcon

Clapper Rail, California race

Snowy Plover

Charadrius alexandrinus 6¼"

Undisturbed sandy coastal beaches are prime nesting areas for Snowy Plovers, but few such places remain because of human activities during the summer breeding season. Fortunately, these plovers are somewhat adaptable, and there have been reports of scattered colonies on sinks, playas, and receding lakeshores in the California interior, where they are less likely to be molested. Nests are mere scrapes in the sand sometimes lined with small pieces of shells. Sexes generally look alike, except that the male's head and shoulder marks are darker and more distinct than those of females and immatures. These birds are often tame and allow close approach; instead of flying, they may run ahead with long strides. They are usually quiet but at times will utter a low musical whistle, *pe-e-et.*

Least Tern

Sterna antillarum 9"

There are only a few nesting colonies of this bird, our smallest tern, remaining in northern California, mainly in the San Francisco Bay area. Favored nesting sites are open sandy or pebbly beaches, either on islands or near the shore above the high-tide line. Numbers of this bird have greatly declined because of disturbance by humans, dogs, and introduced predators. This tern feeds by skimming the surface of the water or by hovering and then diving after tiny fish and crustaceans. Nests are small unlined scrapes in the sand. Winter is spent in Central and South America.

Snowy Plover, female

Least Terns

Yellow-billed Cuckoo   *Coccyzus americanus* 12"

The Yellow-billed Cuckoo requires breeding habitats of tall, dense riparian groves with thick understories. There are only a few suitable localities left in California, mostly along the upper Sacramento River system and the Kern River farther south. There have been reports of a few individuals seen in lower-elevation riparian habitats on the eastern side of the Sierra Nevada. Nests are flimsy affairs built on horizontal limbs of small trees; the young climb with agility about the nesting site shortly after hatching. To prevent extirpation of this species from California, preservation of the remaining riparian habitats is essential. At the Kern River, a breeding-ground restoration program has shown promising results. Winter is spent in South America.

Willow Flycatcher   *Empidonax traillii* 5¾"

Here is another bird with a highly specialized breeding habitat— patches of low, scrubby willows surrounded by meadows and near water. This bird is one of the group of small flycatchers that all look much alike. Habitat destruction, especially in the lowlands, and parasitism by cowbirds are thought to be the main causes of the Willow Flycatcher's decline. In northern California, the largest numbers of nesting Willow Flycatchers are located in montane willow thickets, where cowbird pressure is less severe. Central and northern South America are the primary wintering grounds.

Yellow-billed Cuckoo

Willow Flycatcher

Suggested References

An enormous amount of literature, ranging from very technical to very simple, is available covering almost every facet of ornithology (the study of birds), with more being published every year. Following are a few selections that the beginner, depending on interest, might want to add to his or her library. These books provide details on identification, specifics of life histories, or descriptions of particular birding locations that were not possible to include in this work.

American Ornithologists' Union. 1983. *Check-list of North American Birds*. 6th ed. and subsequent supplements. Washington, D.C.: American Ornithologists' Union. The standard reference for names, classification, and ranges of all species recorded from North America, Central America, and Hawaii.

Clarke, Herbert. 1989. *An Introduction to Southern California Birds*. Missoula, Mont.: Mountain Press. The southern California counterpart to the northern volume.

Ehrlich, Paul, David S. Dobkin, and Darryl Wheye. 1988. *The Birder's Handbook*. New York: Simon & Schuster. Slightly larger than, and a good supplement to, field guides. Includes interesting accounts of most North American birds, concisely arranged.

Gaines, David. 1988. *Birds of Yosemite and the East Slope*. Lee Vining, Calif.: Artemisia Press. Exhaustive discussion, but in a highly readable style, covering the status and distribution of birds in east-central California.

National Geographic Society. 1987. *Field Guide to the Birds of North America*. 2nd ed. Washington, D.C.: National Geographic Society. The best of current field guides, but may be too detailed for beginners.

Peterson, Roger Tory. 1990. *A Field Guide to Western Birds*. Boston: Houghton Mifflin. The standard guide for beginning and intermediate birders.

Roberson, Don. 1985. *Monterey Birds*. Carmel, Calif.: Monterey Peninsula Audubon Society. Thoroughly covers bird distribution in one of California's best birding areas.

Small, Arnold. 1994. *California Birds: Their Status and Distribution.* Vista, Calif.: Ibis Publishing. An extremely detailed account of the distribution of all California's bird species.

Stallcup, Rich. 1990. *Ocean Birds of the Nearshore Pacific.* Stinson Beach, Calif.: Point Reyes Bird Observatory. Includes sea mammals and other wildlife in addition to birds. An entertaining and authoritative guide.

Terres, John K. 1980. *The Audubon Society Encyclopedia of North American Birds.* New York: Alfred A. Knopf. A large book containing a great amount of detailed information in nontechnical language, with many photographs.

Westrich, Lolo, and Jim Westrich. 1991. *Birder's Guide to Northern California.* Houston: Gulf Publishing. Describes and gives directions to many birding areas along with other pertinent information to help the visiting or beginning birder find and enjoy birds in northern California.

Index

Notes:

About the Author

An avid birder since childhood, Herbert Clarke has studied birds all over the world, with special emphasis on California. He is the author of *An Introduction to Southern California Birds* and coauthor of *Birds of the West*. His writings and photographs have appeared in many prestigious books, magazines, and natural history publications. Each year, in addition to his frequent travels, he leads tours, gives illustrated lectures, and instructs classes on birds. Mr. Clarke makes his home in Glendale, California, together with his wife and constant field companion, Olga.